Groundwork

Roger B. Swain

Groundwork

A GARDENER'S ECOLOGY

ILLUSTRATED BY ABIGAIL RORER

HOUGHTON MIFFLIN COMPANY
BOSTON/NEW YORK

For information about permission to reproduce selections from
this book, write to Permissions, Houghton Mifflin Company,
215 Park Avenue South, New York, New York 10003.

For information about this and other Houghton Mifflin trade
and reference books and multimedia products, visit
The Bookstore at Houghton Mifflin on the World Wide Web
at http://www.hmco.com/trade/.

Library of Congress Cataloging-in-Publication Data
Swain, Roger B.
Groundwork : a gardener's ecology / Roger B. Swain.
p.   cm.
Includes bibliographical references (p.   )
and index.
ISBN 0-395-68400-5
ISBN 0-395-71825-2 (pbk.)
1. Gardening — Environmental aspects.   2. Gardening —
Environmental aspects — New England.   3. Garden ecology.
4. Garden ecology — New England.   I. Title
SB454.3.E53S88   1994   93-21444
635′.0974 — dc20   CIP

Printed in the United States of America
Book design by Robert Overholtzer

QUM 10 9 8 7 6 5 4 3 2 1

These essays have appeared in slightly different form
in *Horticulture* magazine.

For sons Robert and Benjamin

The land expects something from us. The line of succession, the true line, is the membership of people who know it.

— WENDELL BERRY

CONTENTS

FOREWORD

The best lessons are accompanied by sweat. What we end up knowing for sure, what proves to be most true, is the things we learned when breathing hard. It's not that old chestnut about success being ten percent inspiration and ninety percent perspiration. The perspiration itself is a source of insight, as if the moisture frees up some gearbox between our ears, allowing our thoughts to move. Practical knowledge, my great-grandfather called it.

I was sixteen years old when I first came to southern New Hampshire, an excited adolescent whose parents had just purchased an abandoned farm. The papers had scarcely been passed before I was out with a spading fork, digging up the icy meadow grass, determined to have ground broken for spring. Now, thirty years later, this is my farm, Elisabeth's and mine, and we have nearly full-grown sons. Though we are considerably wiser, we are no less capable of working up a prodigious sweat. We still try to do more than the days will allow.

Most of our hundred and twenty-five acres are forest. The pastures and fields were abandoned and allowed to grow up to trees long before my family arrived. We manage to keep roughly ten acres open, on both sides of a tar road that bisects the property. At an elevation of eleven hundred feet, this land is too high to be considered prime agricultural ground, but the soil between the rocks is good, and the cold air draining away into the valley on our east gives us a fifth frost-free month.

Neither of us aspires to a life of subsistence. We both have full-time jobs. But this place has become the center of our world. Depending on the season, we are on cherry-picking, potato-digging, cider-pressing time. Keeping it all going has meant examining every activity, looking for ways to do it better. There is something to be said for being chronically short of time and breath. It prompts one to use one's resources wisely. Gardening well means using natural forces to advantage. It means gardening in a way that preserves the integrity of natural communities, that preserves more than the well-being of the gardener.

As our town's population has grown, so have the number of separate properties. By now, ours is one of the larger pieces of land. If we manage to keep it intact, to live here for another thirty years, if our sons grow up knowing how to care for the place, it will be in part because of what we have learned from gardening. In debates over development, wildlife preservation, air and water pollution, we notice that opponents and proponents usually take up positions of strength atop opposing peaks and bombard each other with rhetoric. Gardeners, however, tending the ground in between, are forced to be pragmatic. Gardeners have their fingers on the pulse of nature, and they are accustomed to making choices, living with limits, paying attention to practicality. At least successful gardeners are. Here in New England, with our thin soils, unpredictable weather, and short growing seasons, no one gardens for long unless he or she gardens with a fair amount of what should be called uncommon sense.

I wish to acknowledge the support of my fellow editors at *Horticulture* magazine, as well as the staff of *The Victory Garden* television show, for encouraging me to spend so much time here, and for understanding why I have on more than one occasion yawned and fallen asleep on my office floor after lunch. It is this land, however, to which I am most indebted — for its harvests, its lessons, its beauty, for every sweaty moment in its company.

EDITING LANDSCAPE

Nature writes, gardeners edit. The cleared acre directly across the road from this house is especially fecund land. The patches of club moss and meadow grass are spawning ground for white pine and gray birch. Staghorn sumac stems, like velvet-covered antlers, erupt from the sod, fueled by a common reserve of starch in the roots. Adolescent saplings of swamp maple, chokecherry, and ash rise from the groin of every highbush blueberry. This is pasture headed for the woods. Even the grapevines and Virginia creeper that tangle with the alders in their midst cannot fetter the procreative rush.

It is this very vigor, this muscular exuberance, that makes this such an economical, energy-efficient garden. The plants in this particular plot are all self-supporting, and self-replicating. They look like they belong, because they do. My only input to this landscape has been repeated editing. Without it, of course, the thickets would continue to grow upward. In ten or fifteen years, the view from our kitchen window would be of forest, not of the summit of the small glaciated peak, the monadnock, on whose shoulder we live. Even before that happened, our Sunday supper would be affected, as the rising tide of greenery would shade out the blueberries, cutting into our blueberry pies.

Some people have no taste for this work. A logger I spoke with last summer, standing next to his skidder with its mud-caked wheels, spat and said, "I don't cut brush." I, however, do. Again and again for the past quarter-century I've gone over this ground. It is something that fits in between making maple syrup and sowing peas, something I do when the snow is gone but before the swollen buds leaf out.

I have my own guidelines. I don't want the finished result to be taller than eight or ten feet. Shorter is better. I try to rogue out all the young oaks, ashes, red maples, and chokecherries — their bark and buds a lesson in winter botany. I have seen how quickly these can get out of hand. I also try to nip in the bud the shoots of sumac and poplar. Some of the smaller white pines, however, I leave until they grow too tall. Their long-needled branches are a welcome touch of evergreen in the winter months. Blueberry bushes of any size are sacred. And alders are to be encouraged, both for the nitrogen that is added to the soil by the symbiotic bacteria on their roots and for the well-being of the woodcocks.

The courtship flight of the woodcock is the maddest of spring serenades. Each March we stand on our doorstep after dusk listening for the male. Somewhere off in the gloom he leaps up, spirals hundreds of feet into the air on whistling wings, and zigzags back to the earth like a falling leaf uttering liquid chirps. He utters a nasal *peent* that signals he has landed and is stalking off stiff-legged to join an admiring mate. Both sexes feed in thickets of alder and willow, pushing their long bills full-length into the soft earth and probing with the sensitive, mobile tips for earthworms. But on moonlit March nights, males need clearings like the one across the road, with enough elbow room to launch themselves into love.

Manuscript editors work with scissors, tape, and blue pencils. Landscape editors use pruning shears, long-handled loppers, axes, and handsaws, or at least I do. I pile these tools into an old battered blue wheelbarrow, along with a chainsaw and its accompanying cans of gas and oil. Over the years I have discovered that fewer things get left behind in the undergrowth if I keep everything in this rolling toolbox. On my feet I wear waterproof boots, the better to splash through the vernal pools left by the last of the melting snow.

Most of the cutting I can do with my pruning shears

or the larger loppers. For the thicker pine trunks, I use the handsaw. Pine trees are blessedly easy to dispatch. No matter how big they have grown, if I cut them below the lowest branch they are history. Hardwoods are another matter. Like an author who insists on putting the same bad sentence back into a manuscript, hardwood argues back. Cut a stem, and it resprouts. About the only time that I resort to a chainsaw is when I want to cut some red oak sapling lower to the ground, erasing the evidence that I have already cut it back half a dozen times.

I know I wouldn't have to put up with this if I came back to these stems several times in the course of the summer and rubbed off the young sprouts. Such repeated goatlike grazing will ultimately discourage even the most vigorous oak stump. It will also vanquish sumac and poplars, but only if you have cut every last stem. These species send up suckers from the roots. An entire stand of sumac may be a single plant. Any stem left standing will fuel the regrowth of one that has been cut back. Because I am unwilling to forgo entirely the clusters of fuzzy red fruit and the brilliant fall foliage, I pay the cost.

Don't let me give the impression that what I'm doing is particularly onerous work. In March there are no leaves yet on the brush, no deerflies on the back of my neck. Yes, it would be easier just to let the forest return

— but that wouldn't be gardening. It would be easier, too, to wait until August, when the ground is dry, and ask my neighbor to take his tractor and big rotary mower and grind everything up to coarse green chop. But neither of these would give me such a delicate blend of pussywillows and plum blossoms, wild grapes and ruffed grouse.

So attractive is a garden like this that some people are deliberately planting them, trying to reestablish native plants and their accompanying wildlife. But consider the advantages of doing things my way. I never have to measure the pH of the soil or ask myself whether it is too wet or too dry for a particular species to do well. I don't have to worry about whether this is the right season for transplanting, whether a plant is set too high or too low in the ground, whether its roots are damaged or potbound, whether or not it should be staked. I don't have to worry about hardiness or winterkill. And the price is always right.

Yet despite my hands-off attitude, I can point with pride to the result — a garden that offers year-round pleasure, from winter's red-twigged blueberry bushes and evergreen sheep laurel to the rhodora blossoms and alder catkins of spring, through summer's wild strawberries, milkweed, and goldenrod, and finally on to the fall extravaganza of New England asters beneath the sugar maples.

This is a landscape created by deletion. I cut down a white pine and something takes its place. I cannot guarantee what it will be. It will come on the wind, or the wings of birds, or the tiny feet of a mouse. I can say general things about succession, about how hardwoods replace pines in old New England fields. But what I am maintaining is a state of arrested succession. I am holding this patch of ground midway between hayfield and forest.

The results can be as formal or informal as I choose. If I don't like what springs up in a particular place, I exercise my veto. I now have a line of young sugar maples running perpendicular to the road, trees that will someday be tapped for maple syrup by my children. The straightness of the row leaves no doubt that there was human intervention, but the point is that I didn't do any planting. Over the years, I have simply removed all the trees that germinated out of place.

The distinction is driven home when I go indoors at the end of the day, only to receive a phone call from someone soliciting contributions to pay for the planting of trees to improve the environment. I tell the caller that I have just spent six hours improving the environment by cutting trees down. She hangs up. Maybe she thinks I'm joking. But with the exception of a highly domesticated crop such as corn, which is entirely dependent on human-assisted sowing for its survival, plants do an excellent job of reproducing on their own. It is a small point, but I try not to say that I grow the plants in my various gardens. I raise tomatoes, I raise apples. But the plants themselves do the actual growing.

Those of us who are tending native plants, whether self-sown or deliberately planted, soon discover that they are a pretty undemanding, self-sufficient bunch, capable of being raised without much effort on the gardener's part. This lure of low maintenance is certainly one of the reasons that so many wildflowers are now being offered for sale, with nurseries from New England to California specializing in supplying native species, or at least species that are native to some part of the United States, if not the customer's particular zip code. But purchasing plants and creating a garden for them isn't effortless, nor is it the best way to assure that the rarer, truly endangered species will survive.

Indeed, many wildflowers offered for sale have been dug from the wild. Our temperate native orchids, such as lady's-slipper, fringed orchid, and pogonia, have such a specific dependence on certain species of soil fungi that they have never been successfully raised commercially. Anyone who buys a plant of pink lady's-slipper is acquiring a specimen that has been plucked from its native haunts and will almost certainly die within a few years of transplanting. Even species of trillium that can be raised from seed are so slow-growing (two years to germinate plus five to eight to reach blooming size) that the retail price has to be ten dollars or more to be economical. Many native species can be and are being successfully propagated by nurseries, but environmentally minded gardeners should be sure to ask whether the plants they are buying have actually been nursery propagated. The term "nursery grown" can be misleading, for it includes plants that have been dug in the wild and simply held at the nursery until they are sold.

Research continues on how best to propagate some of the rarer native plants, but nursery propagation and subsequent cultivation will always be a distant second in importance to preserving the native habitat and letting these plants proliferate on their own. Most botanical gardens and wildflower societies are not content simply to showcase the native species being cultivated on their grounds but are actively engaged in land conservation campaigns.

There is an important caveat for anyone trying to restore the natural vegetation to a piece of land, especially if the site has been highly disturbed. Letting nature take its course doesn't always result in the proliferation of indigenous species. On the way to my city office I regularly pass a yard on a broad suburban street that, judging from the forest that encases the house, hasn't been mowed in a long, long time. The elderly woman who lives there, I have been told, is a recluse who has forsworn painting the house, raking the walk, or even picking up her mail. She is, I am sure, a consternation to her neighbors in this elegantly manicured neighborhood, but her yard is a prime example of suburban nature gone rampant. The grove of twenty-five-foot saplings that hides her door is made up wholly of Norway maples. Thick ropes of oriental bittersweet spiral up their branches and drape from trunk to trunk. Mixed into the understory are seedling crab apples, winged euonymus, some struggling forsythias, and a bit of Japanese privet. When I stopped for a close look last fall, *Cynanchum nigrum,* the climbing milkweed or black swallowwort, from Europe, was growing over the remains of the fallen entrance gate. This weed and everything else I spotted are introduced, exotic species. To top it all off, that afternoon the yard was filled with hundreds of birds, their chorus drowning out the lawn service's leafblower down the street. From the sound of it, every last one of them was an English sparrow.

I'm not surprised that the recluse's house is surrounded by Norway maples. Norway maples were introduced to North America in 1870 and planted widely as street trees. They have proved to be one of the hardiest trees in cultivation, possessing a vigor they demonstrate with great crops of seeds and seedlings. Any seedling that is more than a couple of years old is all but impossible to pull out of the ground by hand.

Gardeners have always trafficked in exotic specimens. The Boston ivy that covers the walls of New England colleges is *Parthenocissus tricuspidata,* from Japan. The English, in turn, have fallen in love with our native *Parthenocissus quinquefolia,* the Virginia creeper. Some introduced species prove ill-suited to their new terrain and die off despite the best attention. Others find conditions close enough to their native habitat and survive. A few positively prosper, perhaps because they have escaped from the limits of their traditional pests and diseases. These are the exotic plants that become pernicious weeds. Australian horsetail, Japanese honeysuckle, kudzu, white mulberry, buckthorn, eucalyptus, and gorse — the catalog of exotic nuisances spreads from coast to coast. Many of these are plants we once admired as ornamentals — purple loosestrife, yellow flag, Japanese barberry. Now the problem is too many of them. They have vaulted the garden fence and taken over the countryside. Years ago, I took a state forester up on an offer of a bargain-price bundle of autumn olive seedlings (*Elaeagnus umbellata*) because he said birds would love eating the small red fruits. They do, and I will be dealing with bird-disseminated seedlings of this Himalayan shrub on my land for the rest of my life.

I wish I believed that chemical herbicides were an appropriate weapon in what has become, in many places, a war against invading exotics. Poison ivy may be grounds for chemical warfare, but only in those locations where the vine cannot be appreciated for the native plant it is. In general these phytotoxic chemicals should be used as little as possible, and always in concert with some plan that assures that the gardener won't have to resort to them again. Restricting their use to an absolute minimum will save us from having to worry about accidental injury to other plants, toxic residues in the soil, and the fear that the chemicals may someday prove to have turned and bitten the hand that touched them.

I have, however, just recently expanded my mechanical arsenal. There is a new tool called a Weed Wrench. It was invented in 1988 by a Californian named Tom Ness as a better way to uproot several species of exotic broom that had invaded San Francisco's Golden Gate National Recreation Area. Bright orange and brutally strong, it consists of two jaws that clamp around a plant's trunk and a long lever-arm handle. The jaws give an eighteen-to-one mechanical advantage, the lever arm a six-to-one. In short, the patented Weed Wrench is designed to give ordinary mortals like myself the grip and the back of Hercules. Yes, even my medium-size model weighs a hefty seventeen pounds, but anything that I can get its two-inch jaws around I can wrest from the ground. Nor am I the only person to think this new tool is fantastic. Eager conservationists have been wrenching Brazilian pepper from the Florida Everglades, multiflora rose from midwestern prairies, and Norway and sycamore maples from New York's Central Park.

But no tool, no matter how well designed or how diligently wielded, will ever give us back an undisturbed native flora. The glaciers, native Americans, European colonists, and the USDA have all permanently altered the landscape. Even those restoration managers with a clear vision of what they want to achieve say that their job will never be done. I for one certainly will never be finished cutting brush in New Hampshire. For the day, yes, but not for good. As gardeners we can protect the native plant communities that remain, and we can insist that future mass plantings, whether in city parks or alongside highways, be done with the appropriate native selections. But we must also recognize that the exotic plants that have become naturalized are well on their way to being permanent members of our communities. We have influence. We can assure that the rarer species are not crowded out and lost. But in the end, landscape, like language, has a life of its own.

THE RETURN

OF THE NUTRIENTS

Slash and burn agriculture has its merits. Chop down a piece of forest, set fire to the fallen trunks and limbs, and you will be left with a nutrient-rich ground. In our case, the trees were not the liana-laden buttressed hardwoods of Amazonia but grapevine-covered white pines. Crows, not macaws, perched in their crowns. All one winter we worked in the snow, carving a 150-by-150-foot clearing in the woods. The bigger logs I rolled with a peavey to where I could later square them into beams to build a shed. The branches, oozing pitch from their cut ends, we piled in heaps and burned, warming our hands at the pyre.

The first summer the ground was still dotted with stumps. The corn and beans that we planted around them grew from soil that was thick with the accumulated duff of the forest floor, sweetened and fertilized

with the ashes of our winter's work. Now, ten years later, only a couple of the largest stumps remain. The original leaf mold is long gone, as are the remains of those midwinter bonfires. We still harvest cartloads of vegetables from this ground each year, but only because we have continued to tend the soil.

The road we live on turns off the highway a mile from our house and climbs three hundred feet before it reaches us. We can hear the occasional big truck long before we see it, the labored downshifting as it grinds slowly up the last punishingly steep pitch. There is much to be said for living on a hill. Our growing season is a good six weeks longer than in the valley, where the cold air pools on frosty nights. And we are well out of reach of any floodwaters. But hill farms like ours have one great liability, and that is that over time the soil's fertility gradually slips away.

Part of the problem is gravity. The mineral elements that are essential for the growth of plants are water soluble, and percolating water washes them deeper into the ground or downslope. These nutrients may not leach as rapidly as they do in the case of newly cleared tropical rainforests, where the soil gets a hundred inches or more of rain a year, but the direction is the same. Furthermore, erosion carries away even those nutrients, such as phosphorus, that are comparatively tightly bound to individual soil particles. These are delivered to the alluvial floodplains downstream, in rich layers of silt left behind when the river overflows its banks.

A far greater cause of nutrient loss, however, is the very nature of gardening itself. We cut asparagus, shell peas, pick tomatoes, pull carrots, and dig potatoes. Not to mention the bouquets of flowers we gather or the herbs we dry. And every leaf, flower, stem, or root that we harvest from the garden takes nutrients with it. Each hundred-pound sack of potatoes takes away roughly ten ounces of nitrogen. And the farther away from the garden such nutrients travel, the less likely they are ever to come back. We have successfully trained our friends who leave with the back seats and trunks of their cars full of fresh produce to return the containers — the baskets, flats, and crates. But we have never quite been able to bring ourselves to say that we also need returned what's left after they have eaten the vegetables.

Seventeen different chemical elements have been identified as essential to plant growth. Not all of them are required in equal amounts. Carbon, hydrogen, and oxygen, for example, account for ninety-five percent of the dry weight of any plant and are abundantly provided by the atmosphere. At the other extreme are eight so-called micronutrients that are present in amounts of less than ten parts per million. These are

chlorine, iron, boron, manganese, zinc, copper, molyb-
denum, and, most recently, nickel. If I grew tomatoes
hydroponically I would need to add these trace elements, but anyone who plants in soil that contains
organic matter usually has an ample supply.

The only elements that I, or most gardeners, need
really be concerned about are six so-called macronutri-
ents — nitrogen, phosphorus, potassium, calcium, sulfur, and magnesium. Of these I get to cross half off
my shopping list. The form of ground limestone that
I spread to keep the soil's pH at 6.5 (instead of its
natural 5.0) is powdered dolomite, which contains magnesium in addition to calcium. I may someday need to
add sulfur, but not so long as industrial smokestacks keep
belching the sulfur dioxide that showers down on our
soil as acid rain.

The bags of "complete" fertilizer stacked alongside
the grass seed and dog chow at our local garden supply
store actually contain only three nutrients — nitrogen,
phosphorus, and potassium. These are the elements
that plants are most likely to find lacking, and they are
the ones that form the backbone of the United States
chemical fertilizer industry.

The potassium (whose chemical symbol, K, comes
from the Latin word *kalium,* meaning "alkali") is potassium chloride, also called muriate of potash. It has
been recovered from the brine of Searles Lake, Califor-

nia, or mined near Carlsbad, New Mexico. The phosphorus (P) is a phosphate rock mined in Florida or one of half a dozen other states and treated with sulfuric acid to create superphosphate, which is more water soluble than rock phosphate.

The nitrogen (N) in these bags is the most expensive of the three components, and the one that is most valuable to the gardener. Nitrogen gas, although it makes up seventy-eight percent of the earth's atmosphere, cannot be used by plants until it is "fixed," or combined with oxygen or hydrogen to make compounds such as nitrates or ammonia, which plants can use to synthesize proteins. The principal industrial process for doing this is the Haber process, named for the German chemist who won a Nobel prize in 1918 for its discovery. This synthetic fixation requires energy, lots of it. Twenty-five thousand BTUs go into producing a single pound of nitrogen fertilizer, and nitrogen fertilizer production consumes two percent of the total natural gas used in this country. When you are calculating which of two formulations of fertilizer is the better buy, it is sufficient to determine the relative prices for the nitrogen. The phosphorus and the potassium each contribute less than ten percent of the cost.

I used to buy hundreds of pounds of chemical fertilizer every year. I was a teenager then, just beginning to grow vegetables, and I was gardening by the book, specifically a tattered paperback copy of *The Pocket Book of Vegetable Gardening,* by Charles H. Nissley, extension professor of vegetable gardening at the New Jersey Agricultural Experiment Station. This was the only popular book that I could find at the time, and its copyright was 1942. I bought fertilizer in eighty-pound bags of 10-10-10, secure that I was getting eight pounds of actual N, P, and K in every one. I spread it liberally. "An application of approximately fifty pounds to every 1,000 square feet of garden surface is usually satisfactory," Nissley counseled. I added more for good measure. It was only five dollars a bag, and it seemed better to be safe than sorry. Every time a plant looked a little yellow, I slopped on some more nitrogen. Everything was green, very green. The soil was awash in nutrients.

Yes, there were a few problems. On several occasions I scorched the edges of leaves by applying one drench too many of the soluble salts. And the overabundance of nitrogen kept the bell peppers making leaves when they should have been making flowers. But I went on fertilizing the same way for years before I had any real second thoughts. It was when the per-bag price of fertilizer shot up and never quite came down that I began to try to do things differently.

It wasn't just the talk of nitrates polluting groundwater, or worries that some of our fertilizer was contributing to the algal blooms downstream. It was the realization that the soil in the garden had become distinctly grittier and less friable than when I had first turned it over. It wasn't the garden we have now, south-facing and well drained, but rather a piece of low ground in back of the house. But even here the soil now held water less well and was more prone to crusting. In short, it displayed all the classic symptoms of insufficient organic matter. The realization wasn't an epiphany, mind you. Realizing that I, too, had become a victim of this commonest problem took a couple of years to sink in. But in the end it was no less embarrassing to have been so smitten by the power of a handful of chemicals that I'd neglected the obvious. And when we got around to moving the garden to the better location across the road, cutting down the pines and breaking fresh ground, I resolved to pay more attention to the soil itself.

New ground in this part of the country can contain as much as ten percent organic matter. But cultivation reduces that swiftly. Whether by hand or beast or gasoline tiller, the repeated stirrings of the soil mix in extra air; the result is the same as if you were blowing on a glowing coal. The organic content burns up. You can keep the fire stoked by adding fresh organic matter, but even diligent gardeners can rarely keep the organic content of cultivated ground at more than fifty percent of what it was before they first plunged a spading fork into it.

The organic matter is essential, though, because it is the fuel for the community of microorganisms that inhabits soil. A single teaspoonful of soil may contain five billion bacteria, twenty million filamentous fungi, and a million protozoa. These fix nitrogen from the air, produce organic acids that serve as a solvent for minerals, help roots take up nutrients from the soil, and prey on plant pathogens.

At the same time the organic matter attracts and holds nutrients, reduces leaching losses, binds soil particles into aggregates (producing a good tilth), and soaks up water. In short, organic matter and the microorganisms that live on it are better stewards of soil structure and fertility than any chemical company. Those who feed the soil and let the soil in turn feed their plants are engaged in what can best be called biological gardening.

Resolving to increase the organic matter of soil is easier than actually doing it. Many "organic" gardeners import their organic matter from great distances. But bringing organic matter from tens or hundreds or even thousands of miles away (in the case of peat moss) has always struck me as being scarcely different from trucking in chemical fertilizers from the same distance, as "chemical" gardeners do. A certain amount of moving things from one place to another is inevitable in gardening, but we want to reduce the consumption of fossil fuels that accompanies long-distance transport. We are aiming for a garden fertility as homegrown as the vegetables we harvest.

I won't claim that what I do is appropriate to commercial agriculture. But as a part-time farmer and amateur gardener, I belong to a great guild not bound by market economics. I measure our success in the declining amounts of chemical fertilizer that I add to the garden each year and the bushels of beans, cucumbers, and squash that we harvest nevertheless.

The number-one alternative to chemical fertilizer has always been animal manure. If we had a ready supply, I would happily add half a ton of horse or cow manure per thousand square feet every couple of years. But we don't keep animals. Nor do our nearest neighbors. The days when horsepower also generated horse manure are long gone. There are still riding stables and a few dairies, but none are close. And the manure we would be trucking up this hill would contain a lot of water. Horse manure is sixty percent water, cow manure eighty-five percent. If we were making an outing, we would probably go down to the beach instead and load up on seaweed, an equally old-fashioned source. Washed up on the high-tide line and sun-dried, it is nearly twice as good a source of nutrients per ton as horse manure (and the salt is not a problem).

Instead, we have been turning our attention to homegrown nutrients. The greatest nitrogen-fixing systems on earth are symbiotic bacteria. Chief among these are bacteria in the genus *Rhizobium,* which form nodules on the roots of leguminous plants from alfalfa to peas. Rotating crops with legumes is a practice that dates back millennia. The Greek Theophrastus, in the third century B.C., described how broad beans add fertility to the soil. Planted one year in three, they provide a significant amount of the nitrogen needed for the vegetable crops that follow. The trick is not to try to improve things by adding lots of soluble nitrogen to the soil, because it suppresses the growth of the nitrogen-fixing bacteria.

I also intend to start using legumes not just in rotation but also as an undercrop. Eliot Coleman, the author of *The New Organic Grower,* has been undersowing squash and cabbage with white clover by planting the clover seed four to five weeks after the crop plants are established. The great advantage of this technique is that in northern New England, where Coleman gardens, the plants have time to become established before cold weather sets in and to make a significant contribution as a nitrogen-fixing, overwintering cover crop. At present the only cover crop that we can sow is winter rye, because we wait until we have harvested the last carrots and cabbages. By then it's too cold to plant anything besides this nonlegume.

Cover crops are a source of both nutrients and organic matter, but by themselves they aren't enough to keep the organic content of our gardens as high as it should be. So I prowl our land for caches of ready-to-use organic matter. I scoop up the crumbled remains of a pile of rotted logs, dig black muck and leaf mold out of the channel that runs through the center of our cranberry bog, and salvage the sphagnum that the beavers gather up and use to dam the overflow of our pond. All of this is fair game.

We save the ashes from our wood stoves and spread them on the snow in the early spring to make it melt faster. A pound of wood ashes is the equivalent of two thirds of a pound of ground limestone in terms of raising the pH, so I have to watch that I don't raise the pH above the optimum 6.5. The fresh ashes also contain a certain amount of caustic lye, so I never spread them directly on growing plants.

The merits of using rock phosphate or the more soluble superphosphates are something that I will leave others to debate, noting only that phosphorus doesn't move very fast in the soil, so you have to put it where it's going to be needed. No matter how soluble a particular brand of fertilizer is advertised to be, in acid soils the phosphorus reacts with the first soil particles it encounters and is firmly bound up. This immobility has one advantage: leaching losses are only measurable over periods of fifty to one hundred years. Because phosphate water pollution is caused by surface runoff, I dig in any phosphate that I add.

I mulch everything heavily, in the belief that nature abhors bare ground and that this is how wild plants get their compost. Part of our garden gets pine needles, raked from beneath the pines. There is no need to worry about them lowering the pH of the soil. We have a friend who mulched with nothing but pine needles for twenty years and never changed her pH an iota. Besides, I'd be happy to have an excuse to add more potassium-rich wood ashes. We also mulch with shredded leaves, cartloads of which we rake up from under the apple trees each fall for the primary purpose of controlling apple scab. Anytime that I can do two good things for the labor of one I think I'm on to something.

Our principal mulch is hay. Bales of mulch hay, once a waste product, have by now become nearly as expensive as new bales. And they are considerably heavier and moldier. So we make our own. We don't bale our hay, we just cut it. We have a small gasoline-powered sickle-bar mower, but we use a scythe when it won't start. We let the cut hay dry in the sun for a while to lighten the load, or just rake it right away if we are in a hurry. We pitch the loose stems into a hand cart, tucking the corners in the way that people did when this was the only way to move hay. In order to end up with the equivalent of an inch of baled hay covering a one-thousand-square-foot garden surface, you need three to five thousand square feet of hayfield. If it's average hay, you are getting twenty-five, ten, and forty pounds of NPK per ton. If it's good legume hay, you are getting fifty pounds of actual nitrogen. Some of this becomes available to soil organisms immediately, the rest in the year that the mulch takes to break down. By spring, what's left of the preceding year's mulch is easy to incorporate into the upper top few inches. I dig it in chiefly to encourage the soil to warm up in the spring, but other gardeners just leave the mulch where it is, knowing full well that nature feeds from the top down.

As for our compost heaps, those piles of garden waste, we no longer locate them off to one side of the garden. Why risk letting nutrients leach into nongarden soil, or having tree rots invade their heart? We build our compost piles right where we garden. That way, too, we don't have far to carry either the ingredients or the finished product. These aren't scientifically prepared piles. We've never been in a rush to make fast compost, the kind that heats up and pasteurizes itself, so we have never paid much attention to carbon-nitrogen ratios. But we are very good about adding everything to them. From the first rhubarb leaves to the last frosted tomato vines cut off their poles, we pile any and all scraps of loose vegetation into a heap. We add rotten apples, sods, ashes, even meat scraps, lobster shells, and the occasional dead woodchuck (what better place to assure that what has been feeding on the garden will in turn feed it?). It takes a year for such a pile to become compost. Whenever we tear one apart, we reserve any undecayed remains to start the next piles. The rest we eagerly add to the garden beds. Both the nature of composting itself — incredible shrinking heaps — and the enormous value of the resulting partially decayed organic matter means that no one ever has too much, or even enough.

I don't suppose we will ever return to the time when lilacs were planted around every outhouse and hogs rooted beneath the wooden seats, their more efficient digestion enabling them to use as food half of what humans excreted and convert the remainder to pig manure. But we are proud of the Clivus Multrum, a Swedish composting toilet, that we use. From its enormous white tank in our cellar we periodically retrieve five-gallon pails of a rich organic brew that would make any Chinese gardener envious. The problems of heavy metal contamination in sewage sludge vanish when you don't mix your sewage with the effluents of industry.

Our friends in the city say that they envy us our freedom here, our opportunities to try new ways to shorten and tighten the nutrient loop. The city does force people to garden in tighter quarters. But we can't help noticing that some of the people who envy us our hayfield and pine grove are still raking up their leaves every fall, bagging them in plastic, and putting them out on the curb for the city to collect. Six months later they are buying back plastic bags filled with organic matter in the form of peat moss. Concerns over municipalities' refusal to collect "yard waste" vanish if you recognize that there really isn't any such thing. Municipal composting programs, as admirable an alternative to landfills as they may be, would all be rendered unnecessary if homeowners could be persuaded not to throw away their organic matter in the first place.

The proper place for organic matter to end its days is at home, not in the outskirts of some distant dump, no matter how well managed it is. I like to think of piles of leaves or brush or compost heaps as borning rooms. There was a time when every New England home had one, a small room next to the chimney where babies were delivered and the dying spent their last days. Childbirth and death were properly consid-

ered home matters, and those lying close by the kitch-
en could be easily cared for. These stores of organic
matter don't have to be right in view, but they should
be kept close to hand. They represent a central principle in the quest for sustained fertility. There is no
need to welcome back nutrients when you haven't said
goodbye.

....

BOTH ENDS OF THE HOSE

Map number 491 in my copy of the *Climatic Atlas of the United States* has a line marked "100 percent" that cuts across New England, passing directly over this house. The line denotes the "ratio of precipitation to evaporation for the normal frost-free season." What it means is that despite the briefness of our summers and the rockiness of our soil, we live in a place blessed with all the rainfall our gardens need.

But even here, with some forty inches of annual precipitation, we know just how fickle its delivery can be. We have had winters that were so dry the air filled with fine brown dust, and others so wet that our big chimney spouted sooty streams from between its bricks. Although our state is famous for its skiing, there have been winters with so little natural snow that cross-country equipment could be found at every yard sale.

With weather this capricious, about the only thing

we can trust is that there will come a point each summer when the cucumbers start hollering for a drink. It won't matter that we had a frog-choking deluge three weeks earlier and might get another any day now. Unless the vines get watered right away, the developing fruits will end up misshapen and bitter. What the map in the *Climatic Atlas* describes as a balance between precipitation and evaporation is in reality a flood and a drought going hand in hand. And this brings me to the state of our plumbing.

Plumbing is the real heart of country living. It is as vital, as delicate, and as hidden as the organ that circulates human blood, yet it is scarcely ever discussed. The lifestyle magazine writers certainly never mention it, nor do the real estate agents. But for every bowl of homegrown strawberries, for every swim in the pond, for every night out watching the Perseids, there is time that must be spent in the cellar. The Maine humorist John Gould once explained that he missed a summer altogether because he was down in his cellar at the time, fixing his pump. All sorts of things — electrical outages, sand, mud, dead leaves, air bubbles, and leaky fittings — can stay the water from its appointed rounds.

When you are the one in charge of the family waterworks, as I am, you don't lie awake at night wondering whether the car is locked up or the front door is closed. The real concerns are the well's going dry and the leach field's failing. Such responsibilities confer a special respect for this odorless, tasteless, colorless liquid, and make us more than a little careful how we use it. We are not alone in this. A study of water consumption in Ipswich, Massachusetts, found that houses connected to city services used twenty-seven percent more water than those with self-contained plumbing. This is no surprise. There's nothing like having to haul water from the nearest stream by the bucketful, at 8.3 pounds per gallon, to make you quick to turn off the faucet.

Because we don't have a water meter, we don't know precisely how much water we take from our fieldstone-lined well. But it is probably on the low side of the forty to seventy gallons per person per day that most Americans use. In the summer, though, everyone uses more. Easterners, with our summer thunderstorms, overcast days, and cooler temperatures, may use ten to a hundred gallons more a day. In some parts of the western United States, however, people draw an extra hundred to two hundred gallons a day, and the tripled usage puts a tremendous strain on municipal water budgets.

Nearly all of this extra water goes to irrigating lawns and gardens. Some three quarters of our nation's total outside usage goes to keeping grass green. The "inch of water per week" that all the gardening texts so glibly

recommend adds up to six hundred and twenty-five gallons for every thousand square feet. And those misguided or mistimed sprinklers — the ones wetting down the street and the sidewalk, making midday rainbows in the sunlight — are delivering only a fraction of the water they emit to the lawn itself. Most is going down the storm drains or evaporating before it even hits the ground.

There is no question that plants need lots of water. It is their principal ingredient — up to eighty percent or more of the fresh weight in most instances. Some plant parts are wetter still. The water contents of tomatoes, lettuce, and cucumbers, for example, are ninety-four, ninety-five, and ninety-six percent, respectively. One function of water is to keep a plant's temperature down on hot days by serving as both a heat sink and an evaporative coolant. Water also keeps the tissues turgid, providing a rigidity to the cells that is especially important in supporting herbaceous leaves and stems. And water carries substances within the plant, transporting sugars in the sap, moving dissolved minerals up from the soil. As if that weren't enough, water is part of photosynthesis itself. When water and carbon dioxide are combined in the presence of light to yield glucose and oxygen, it is the water molecules that are split and that give off the oxygen.

For every single pound of dry matter that a plant

produces, it takes in some three hundred to five hundred pounds of water, losing ninety-seven to ninety-nine percent of it by transpiration through the leaves. Over a six-month growing season, a mature apple tree needs an estimated eighteen hundred gallons of water. On a single sunny day in mid-August, the vegetable garden may use up a gallon of water per square yard. Although plants can all deal with periods of water shortage by closing their stomata (the tiny openings in their epidermis through which water vapor and other gases pass), this cuts off the supply of carbon dioxide needed for photosynthesis. You can't have growth without water. It is no different for green plants than it is for municipalities.

Prior to 1940 no one did much watering of lawns, not in the more humid parts of the country. With the increased availability of piped municipal water, with the invention of convenient, low-cost sprinklers, and with a new vision of community beautification, outdoor faucets were turned on full. Continued population growth and wasteful watering practices have finally collided head on. Whether the consequence is a falling reservoir or rising water bills, water conservation has become an issue from coast to coast. For gardeners it means paying attention to both ends of the hose.

Though we have our own well, like everyone else in this town, we have come perilously close to running out of water more than once. As summer progresses we record the falling water level by dropping a tape measure from the crossbeam in the well-house roof until we hear it splash — 108 inches, 109 inches, 110.5 inches. The numbers shape our future, for as our neighbor Jim Whitney warned us our first summer, the wells here don't rise until deer hunting season — the first of November.

The annual decline of the water level in our dug well, however, is only one of the reasons that we don't try to water the garden from it except in emergencies. Another is the fact that ours is a gravity-feed system that delivers water downhill without a pump. It does not, however, deliver water with enough pressure to power a sprinkler head, or even, for that matter, to supply a second-floor bathroom. But the third reason is that it seems foolish to be using water of this quality — water that has been covered and screened, water that is free of algae and pollen, water in which no frogs have swum or birds have waded — for something as prosaic as wilty petunias and thirsty celery.

Instead, the water we irrigate with comes from a parallel plumbing system. This one draws water from an old concrete reservoir in front of the barn, which we replenish from an intermittent stream that flows past one end. In a sense, this is one large rain barrel and the stream is a gutter that drains into it via a downspout. An electric pump then sucks water from this reservoir and delivers it through a plastic pipe to the garden. (In theory this is how it works. In practice the pump loses its prime, the intake filter gets clogged, couplings spring leaks, and someone drives the tractor over a line, crushing it flat.) The water that emerges from the sprinkler heads or hose ends isn't polluted, it's just second quality. If you were to hold a glass of it up to the light, you'd see small things swimming around. Not great for drinking, but perfectly fine for plants.

Were we living on an even tighter water budget, we would be tempted to set up yet a third system — one that used secondhand water, water that had already been used for washing in the bathroom sink or shower, or for doing the laundry. The official term for this is gray water, which distinguishes it from black water, the effluent of toilets and the grease- and food-laden water from the kitchen sink. Until recently, using such water for irrigation was universally forbidden by the Uniform Plumbing Code, but in the depths of the last drought in California, during 1989 and 1990, both Santa Barbara and San Luis Obispo officially sanctioned its use. One of the gray-water pioneers is Robert Kourik, whose *Gray Water Use in the Landscape* was one of the first underground guides to designing and installing your own home system, with advice on just what kinds of soaps and detergents to use. Kourik himself, who lives in Santa Rosa, California, and uses thirty gallons of water a day, manages to keep his eight-hundred-square-foot garden irrigated entirely with his own gray water. Spurred by such examples, and by Appendix W, "Gray-water Systems for Single Family Dwellings," which has been passed as an amendment to the 1994 Uniform Plumbing Code, more and more people are now install-ing gray-water systems. Individual homeowners, how-ever, should first check local ordinances to ascertain the current status of regulations in their area.

The hitch is that to be used safely, gray water must be run into a series of mini leach fields where it won't puddle, where only plant roots can get at it. "Avoiding daylighting" is how sanitation engineers put it, refer-ring to the fact that you shouldn't be able to see even a damp spot on the surface. And you must keep mov-ing the connections around, so that no single leach field gets all the effluent all the time. And when rain saturates the soil, you must switch your piping over so the gray water flows into the regular sewage treatment system again.

Personally, since I already have two plumbing sys-tems, I'm reluctant to add a third. So for the moment I'm concentrating on the other end of the hose. *Xeri-scaping* is the new word for not an entirely new idea. Coined within the past ten years, xeriscaping comes from the Greek word *xeros,* meaning "dry," and refers to landscaping that conserves water and protects the environment or, conversely, to water conservation through the creative use of plants. It does *not* mean a landscape that requires no supplemental water at all or a landscape that consists primarily of cactus and rocks.

Planning, not plumbing, is at the heart of xeriscaping. This is especially important with new construction, when people are hurrying to restore the vegetation that the bulldozer scraped away. A few hours or a day spent deciding which zones will be moderate water zones, which will be low water ones, and which will be very low water ones (where supplemental water is used only for establishing new plants) will pay off handsomely in terms of irrigation ease and efficiency. Even in an established landscape, it makes sense to locate the vegetable garden close to the house so that both the hose and the person carrying the fresh-picked corn have a minimal distance to run. In our landscape, where we have let nature do much of the planting, the plants are already grouped according to their moisture needs — such as the stand of sedges, blue flag, and joe-pye weed growing in the damp swale across the road from the house.

In addition to the importance of initial planning and design, the basic principles of xeriscaping are soil analysis, efficient irrigation, practical turf areas, mulches, and, finally, appropriate maintenance. It's not a very sexy list of recommendations; just think of them as a country doctor's advice for avoiding water bills.

Certainly our own approach to watering lawns can't be beat. We don't do it. In this we are just turning the clock back fifty years, since our grandparents didn't either. Yes, the grass does turn straw-colored during long dry spells, but grass has evolved to deal with such events. The prairies of the Great Plains are proof of that. The natural vegetation in our part of the world is woods, not grassland. Our lawns are in infinitely greater danger of being shaded out by trees than they are of dying of thirst. Grass that loses its green isn't dead, it's dormant. Farmers may complain about losing a second cutting of hay to feed their cows. But why should homeowners, who have no market for grass clippings, go to such lengths to keep their lawns growing in high gear all summer long?

Newly seeded or sodded lawns, however, are a different matter. They must have ample water, and for this reason we have always put off lawn repair until late August or early September. Then the young seedlings or the sods are growing on into cooler, damper weather rather than the hotter, drier conditions they would face in the spring. Spring-planted grass almost always needs supplemental watering, fall-planted grass almost never.

The time and effort we save by not watering our lawns we put into soil improvement. Both the texture and the structure of a soil influence how much water it will hold. Soil texture refers to the sizes of individual particles. The larger the particles, the faster the soil drains and the less water it retains. Thus clay and silt soils hold more water than coarse sand. Soil structure, in contrast, refers to the way in which individual soil particles are grouped together. A soil that forms stable crumbs does not become compacted and offers ample pore space for root growth, aeration, and water storage. Wherever possible we dig in manure, compost, or any other partially decomposed organic matter. Up to ten pounds per square yard per year isn't too much on coarse sandy ground. The result can be a doubling or more of the soil's water-holding capacity, not to mention the other attendant benefits. With a greater reserve for plants to draw on between rainfalls, it will be longer before the roots exhaust the available moisture and the leaves wilt.

Still another technique for saving water is to give the plants enough room to develop large root systems. Those highly admired high-intensity gardening techniques, with very close spacing of plants, also require close attention to the watering. Cauliflower, a notoriously sensitive plant when it comes to water shortages, has been experimentally shown to benefit from irrigation when spaced twenty-four inches apart but not when spaced thirty-six inches apart. Desert-dwelling plants frequently space themselves still farther apart, the intervening no-plant's-land serving as the minimum watershed necessary for each specimen.

A corollary of wider spacing is deeper rooting. Because of a lack of oxygen, roots will not grow into soil that is periodically inundated. But if the soil is naturally well drained, or has drains installed, or is heaped up into raised beds, then the roots of plants can penetrate deeper for water. Given suitable conditions, most plants will send down roots four to six feet. The roots of perennial alfalfa have been shown to go down as far as twenty-five feet.

Where we have already planted things, it is too late to amend the soil itself, but we can mulch. Mulch slows the evaporation of moisture from the soil, but even more important, it prevents the growth of weeds that compete for the available water. We try never to have the soil bare for long — no longer than it takes to sow seeds and for the seedlings to sprout. Whether the mulch we use is an impervious, soil-warming one like black plastic film or a cooling, porous layer of pine needles or wood chips depends on whether we will spread it under muskmelon vines or blueberry bushes. But any mulch is better than no mulch at all.

Taken together, these approaches have greatly reduced the number of times that we have to turn on our outside faucets each summer. But there will always be days when, despite the planning, the soil preparation, the spacing, and the mulching, the garden or a part of it needs watering. Then, the more accurately we can deliver the water, the sooner we can turn the water off, and the less of it we will end up using. Soaker hoses are better than sprinklers because they lose less to evaporation. Drip or trickle irrigation is more economical still.

But in terms of ease and evenness of application, nothing will ever match rain. Rain falls so evenly, wetting the lawn, the vegetable garden, the flower border, the fruit trees, and the forest. Downpours are such democratic events. If only we knew how to call them up. Scheduling a picnic, or starting to work on the roof, or sunning the bedsheets sometimes does the job. The rainclouds sweep suddenly out of nowhere, as if they had been waiting for a signal. Then, giddy with pleasure at being able to turn our backs on the plumbing, at least for now, we stand at the windows and watch the rain fall, the earth drinking in the water.

LOSING GROUND

W̲e had better find a way to grow things in asphalt before we cover the world with it." One of these moonless nights, someone ought to emblazon this message in fresh paint across the billboard that announces yet another discount shopping mall down the road. This small act of ecological vigilantism would at least call attention to the huge pile of dark loam that the bulldozers have scraped up. I don't know where the topsoil is headed, only that someday soon it will be trucked away and scattered. Never again will it see long rows of corn on a warm August night, or smell of freshly baled hay. In its place will be acres of hot asphalt, additions to the seven hundred thousand that we already use in this country just for parking our cars.

They call it strip development, this long line of auto dealerships, fast-food franchises, and factory outlets flanking the highway. But each new construction project begins with strip mining. The diesel machines that clank across the fields make short work of a long history. Every inch of topsoil curling up before their polished steel blades took hundreds of years to form. The memories of pioneers, of oxen and axes, of the first tractors, of pick-your-own gladioli and strawberries get torn up and mixed. There is good money in screened loam. Sold by the cubic yard, most of it gets spread in a very thin veneer on the yards of new homes and condominiums.

Some two and a half million acres of arable land in this country are lost each year to the construction of homes, businesses, and highways. So it is not surprising that builders keep turning celery beds into convenience stores and peach orchards into subdivisions. Cropland is twice as likely as noncropland to be urbanized. Most of our nation's cities were founded on flat river-bottom land where the soil was deep and fertile and where there was an ample supply of water. As the population of cities has grown, so has their metropolitan girth. Year by year, the fertile land in their vicinity is gradually surrounded, overshadowed, and finally smothered beneath layers of concrete, asphalt, rock, and brick.

The edge of development sweeping up this particular valley will be at our doorstep in a few years, driven by the inexorable growth of the human population —

ninety-five million additional mouths per year at last count. Anytime that a family decides to have a third child, whether it is in a thatch-roofed hut with a dirt floor halfway around the world or in a fully applianced, center-entrance Colonial with master bathroom just across town, it tightens the screw of development on wild land everywhere. It won't be the steep wooded slopes on this property that the developers will eye first, or the brook cascading over rocky ledges. As the tax assessors already know, the most attractive land is the portion near the road, the part that is smooth and relatively level.

Some of our land is clear; the rest has grown up to trees. But even in the part covered by white pines, you can see by the smoothness of the ground beneath the trees that this soil was once plowed. The cultivation has eliminated the characteristic mounds and pits, the so-called pillows and cradles, that you find where the ground has never been tilled. These little piles of soil beside equal-sized craters result when trees are uprooted by windstorms. Though they can persist in the woods for as long as five hundred years, they are erased by even a single plowing.

Not only are these acres smooth, but they are also relatively free of rock, which is something of an anomaly in this glaciated terrain. Great gray stone walls and broad middens of smaller stones mark the periphery of these acres, testifying that they are not as our forebears found them. When I chose to site my own gardens here, I was taking advantage not only of the topography but of generations of rock-picking. When push comes to shove and I must face the developers directly, it won't be simply the well-being of future generations that will be on my mind, but the ghosts of gardeners past, for surely they hear the ominous advance of the earthmovers even more clearly than I.

The high-calorie, high-protein diet that most of us in this country enjoy requires roughly one and a quarter acres of land per person. Thus I am under no illusion that the quarter-acre of vegetables that I raise each year, or my modest orchard and vineyard, is making an enormous contribution to the nation's larder. But it wouldn't be hard for someone to raise a great deal more on this land. At the height of the World War II Victory Garden movement in 1944, some twenty million back-yard gardeners raised an astonishing forty-four percent of the fresh vegetables in the United States. This would not have been possible, however, without the availability of land. What I see happening to the soil around me and what I read is happening elsewhere makes it seem vitally important to care for land, so that at some point in the future it can be more intensively cultivated.

It's not just development that convinces me that

SUBSCRIBE
& SAVE!

BUSINESS REPLY MAIL

FIRST-CLASS MAIL   PERMIT NO. 22   TAMPA FL

POSTAGE WILL BE PAID BY ADDRESSEE

MARTHA
STEWART **Living**

PO BOX 61891
TAMPA FL 33661-1891

such a need will arise sooner than we think. Each year this country loses some five billion tons of topsoil to erosion, eighty percent of it washed away, the rest blown away. This amounts to the equivalent of about seven inches of topsoil from five million acres. Over the past two hundred years we have managed to lose roughly one third of the topsoil on the nation's croplands, and despite our best efforts at soil conservation, we continue to lose topsoil eight to ten times as fast as it is being formed. Agricultural productivity has continued to increase during this period, but it has done so by dramatically increasing agricultural additions such as nitrogen fertilizer to soils and by abandoning land that has become too badly damaged. Neither trend can continue indefinitely.

Anyone who has ever stood on the rim of the Grand Canyon has a vivid image of what moving water can do. A mile deep and four to eighteen miles wide, this gully was carved by the Colorado River, whose name refers to the red sediment it carries. Just as dramatic are the stark photographs of the Great Plains taken during the Dust Bowl years of the 1930s, when a single four-day windstorm could transport three hundred million tons of soil some fifteen hundred miles east, darken the skies of New York, Baltimore, and Washington, and drop dirt not only on the president's desk in the White House but on the decks of ships three hundred miles out to sea. However, the word *erosion* shares the same Latin root as *rodent,* meaning "to gnaw away." Most erosion is so subtle that most of us scarcely notice it happening.

Erosion is the little dust devil, a tiny tornado, that carries bits of dry grass and grit across a yard. Erosion is the thin stream of muddy water flowing in a road-side ditch after a downpour. Even a single raindrop hitting bare earth has enough force to splash parti-cles of soil. When we wash our freshly picked lettuce, much of the soil we are rinsing off was thrown there by falling water.

Raindrops fall at roughly twenty miles an hour; someone has calculated that the kinetic energy gener-ated by a two-inch rainfall is enough to raise a seven-inch layer of topsoil three feet. Not all of this energy actually goes into moving soil, but some of it does. And on ground with a ten percent slope, sixty percent of the soil is thrown downslope, while only forty per-cent splashes up. We clearly see the consequences of this in our older garden beds. Years ago we left strips of grass running across the slope between individual rectangles of tilled earth. Today these are grassy slopes between level terraces. This sheet erosion, as it is called, has thinned the layer of the topsoil at the top of each bed and thickened it at the bottom.

There are many ways to lessen erosion. Basically, all involve reducing the force of wind and water so that it does not exceed the anchoring or protective forces that are keeping soil in place. Windbreaks shield ground for a distance roughly twenty times their height. And at our northern latitude we value them as well for the protected microclimate they offer tender plants on the leeward side. Keeping the organic content of the soil high creates aggregates that are less easily moved. We also try to leave soil bare as little as possible. Not only do mulches and cover crops save on weeding and fertilizing, they absorb the impact of falling water, slow it down, and allow it to soak into the ground rather than race across the surface. The messages of the Soil Conservation Service, on everything from contour plowing to stubble mulching, aren't applicable only to large-scale commercial acreage. A ten-foot furrow of potatoes running down a gentle slope is enough to demonstrate gullying and rapid soil erosion.

Preserving topsoil means keeping it in place, and it means keeping this soil clean. Soil should never be treated as dirt. Unfortunately, in many places it has become irrevocably contaminated. One of the most serious contaminants is lead. Soils adjacent to older buildings may contain dangerous levels of lead, thanks to years of flaking of lead-based exterior paints. Other soils were contaminated long ago by the use of lead- and arsenic-based pesticides. Gardeners who are purchasing soil to augment their supply should ask for soil that has been tested and found free of such poisons. One of the current major threats to soil is the improper disposal of used motor oil. Last year alone, do-it-yourself oil changers dumped some hundred and seventy-five million gallons of used motor oil, more than sixteen times the amount that was spilled by the wreck of the *Exxon Valdez*.

Some of the pollution of soil is, if not accidental, at least inadvertent. Who would have thought that what one homeowner considered the perfect place to dump waste chemicals, behind the garage, would be someone else's idea of a perfect place to plant tomatoes? Part of the attractiveness of the raised bed approach to gardening, in which individual beds are set off and given a designated frame of planks, stones, or just well-defined paths, is that the soil within is so clearly designated as garden space. Even after years of disuse, such ground should be clearly identifiable. This may not inspire new owners to start tending the ground again, but it may at least persuade someone not to dump on it.

This general problem of saving arable land not only for the present but for future use is on many gardeners' minds today. One of the problems is the hyperinflation of land values that has occurred in the past fifteen or so years, especially in the case of land located within a few hours' drive of metropolitan areas. Val-

ues have appreciated so rapidly that the heirs to any
but the smallest pieces of land are increasingly likely
to have to sell a portion, or indeed the whole estate,
simply to pay the inheritance taxes. Many landown-
ers living an otherwise modest existence have been
shocked to discover that the government considers
them land millionaires. No longer can property simply
be left to the children. This is the path that leads
inexorably to Orchard Estates or Mill Farm Condominiums.

Saving arable land for perpetuity requires legal planning. Unfortunately, lawyers are much more accustomed, and better equipped, to advise clients on how
to hand down the family business than they are to
guide the inheritance of family land. But there are an
increasing number of legal options for those wishing
to protect land from development. Chief among these
is a so-called conservation easement. This is a recorded
deed restriction in which the development rights for
a particular plot of land are given up for perpetuity.
Every easement has to be custom designed. The owner
may want to specify certain agricultural practices or
certain kinds of forestry, for example, or allow for the
building of a new barn but ban the construction of
additional houses or roads. These easements, prepared
after lengthy discussion with lawyers and planners, are
turned over to one of the eight hundred or so land

trusts in this country, nonprofit organizations that enforce the agreed-upon restrictions.

Because such easements usually dramatically cut the valuation of the property in terms of its potential development, they lower the burden of estate taxes and may offer some income tax benefits or reduced property taxes as well. Such easements are different from the current-use classification, which various states have introduced to lower the valuation and property taxes paid for agricultural land. These are temporary restrictions on development, whereas conservation easements are permanent ones. While difficult and expensive to prepare, conservation easements are one way to assure that arable land can remain in private ownership.

In some cases, it is not just good gardening land that the owners wish to preserve but the actual arrangement of the garden itself. The Garden Conservancy, an organization founded in 1989, inspired by the National Trust in Great Britain, is proposing to identify outstanding ornamental gardens and assist their owners in opening them to the public. Turning a private garden into a public one can be a difficult undertaking; the Garden Conservancy assists with plans for horticultural management, legal arrangements, and fund-raising strategies to assure an endowment, and helps in forming or encouraging local support groups. While the conservancy has selected only half a dozen gardens to date, most notably the John Hay Estate in Newbury, New Hampshire, and the Ruth Bancroft Garden in Walnut Creek, California, both the need and the enthusiasm for future assistance remain great.

The most embattled gardeners of all, the ones who live daily with the hot breath of development on their necks, are urban gardeners, those who raise their flowers and vegetables within sight of skyscrapers and highrise apartment houses. Many of their gardens were founded during the 1970s on vacant lots, land created in the heart of many cities by misguided urban renewal, which more often than not took the form of urban removal. For the residents of nearby neighborhoods, many of whom had recently arrived from rural areas, the new patches of land provided an opportunity to continue raising some of their own food.

Clearing the rubble, importing topsoil, and establishing gardens were difficult enough; more difficult still has been the task of defending the ground from developers seeking to put up new housing and other buildings. In downtown Boston, there used to be an exemplary little community garden where Chinese- and English-speaking gardeners worked side by side, sharing a common language. The productivity of some of those tiny plots was astounding. Beds of pak choi were crowded in with trellises of snow peas and long cucumbers. One gardener nurtured basketball-size winter melon, the fruit carefully camouflaged by sheets of newspaper. Though these particular gardens repeatedly won prizes for being among the best in the city, neither their verdure nor the pride of their caretakers was enough to ensure their survival, and today a multiunit housing complex occupies the site.

Such outcomes have taught community garden advocates in Boston and across the country the importance of hitching their cause to the political muscle of other community organizations. Rather than boycotting the meetings of developers, they now attend and patiently, or not so patiently, explain that vacant land that has a garden on it isn't vacant. They point out that community gardening fosters connections among people of widely different cultures, languages, and economic status. More than anything else, they emphasize that gardens can't be located just anywhere. It isn't acceptable for a developer simply to promise land someplace else in exchange for building on a particular parcel. Urban gardens need a constituency in their immediate neighborhood. Nowhere is it clearer that gardens and people go hand in hand. Nowhere is it clearer that the crops being raised are the people themselves.

ARSENIC AND OLD PLASTIC

At this northern latitude, the maples in the swamps have begun turning red by the time we slip the first fully ripened muskmelons from our vines. This is our most impressive achievement, raising these heat-loving fruits on a hill where people come in summer to enjoy the cool days and cooler nights. The taste of a muskmelon that is dead ripe, the flesh translucent and starting to ferment, is both intoxicating and addictive. To grow such melons once is to be bound and determined to do it again.

But how, without a greenhouse, in a part of New England where frost is possible eleven months of the year, does one make this native of West Africa feel at home? The answer is plastic. A mulch of clear polyethylene film beneath the vines raises the temperature of the soil at the roots. And a covering of spun-bonded polyester warms the air around the young foliage. Without plastic, any planting of melons would be a gamble; with it, the fruits become close to a sure thing. But the kudos we receive each September from friends and neighbors sampling our success only make us more conscious of the costs of such artifice.

The issue isn't our tampering with the climate. Gardeners have been doing that for centuries. The emperor Tiberius supposedly had fresh cucumbers on his table every month of the year by having them grown in baskets of rotting manure covered with thin, transparent plates of *lapis specularis,* or talc. Orangeries for overwintering citrus were fashionable in England in the early 1600s and were among the progenitors of the modern greenhouse. And I have a photograph taken at the turn of this century in a melon house on a private estate in America; each fruit is suspended in its own mesh hammock beneath the glass roof.

It is when I am cleaning up the garden after the first frost that I have second thoughts. The crumpled and blackened vines go onto the compost heap to rot away, and the myriad small stones that held the plastic down get piled for next year's use. But the plastic is neither vegetable nor mineral. For a substance to biodegrade, microorganisms have to reduce it eventually to carbon dioxide, water, and inorganic ash. This polyethylene mulch only photodegrades. Another summer's sunlight would cause some of the sheets to shatter into small pieces, which would then blow about the garden or

get mixed into the soil. Our plastic breaks up, but it doesn't break down.

This was not an issue for the pioneers of plastic. The focus in the early days, shortly after World War II, was on how well melons, cucumbers, peppers, and eggplants did when grown in the stuff. Black plastic proved to have all the moisture-retaining and weed-suppressing properties of the traditional organic mulches, and at the same time it warmed the soil beneath by three to five degrees, to the obvious betterment of certain crops. Clear plastic turned out to be even better, warming the soil some seven to ten degrees, if you could control the weeds.

This focus on improved production continues today. University of New Hampshire professor Brent Loy has developed an infrared transmitting mulch (called IRT-76) that blocks photosynthetically active wavelengths of light but transmits the near-infrared, thus preventing weed growth while still warming the soil. Otho Wells, a colleague of Loy's, has been perfecting the use of plastic for row covers, mini-greenhouses constructed over the plants in the garden to retain heat, exclude insects, and offer protection from frost.

The plastic I lay over my melons each spring is a spun-bonded (nonwoven) polyester that weighs less than half an ounce per square yard, a gossamer film that can rest directly on the leaves. It lets light and rain pass through, but not cucumber beetles, and it provides two to three degrees of frost protection. Its greatest virtue, however, is that it raises the daytime temperature ten to twelve degrees above ambient, which is especially valuable in our cool, cloudy days of early summer. After six weeks I have to take it off, because the temperature inside gets close to a hundred degrees, too hot even for melons, and because I need to let the bees pollinate the flowers. But with the combination of clear plastic mulch (plus a little hand-weeding) and the floating row cover I can perform magic, waiting to sow my melon seeds directly in the garden in early June and still pulling off a harvest.

For all its virtues, though, plastic has its dark side. By fall the mulch is no longer a clean, lightweight, virgin sheet. It has turned to yards of cold, wet, dirty junk. We roll it all up each year, tie the rough bales with twine, and load them into the garden cart to take back to the shed, where they wait to go to the dump.

What bothers me about throwing the old plastic away is that it was manufactured from natural gas, that burying it in landfills takes up precious space, and that a thing of so much substance should be useful for something.

I was raised to believe that if you kept things around long enough, you'd find a use for them. My wife, Elisabeth, though, regularly points out that we are running out of space. She points to the plastic mulch that hasn't yet made its way to the dump and the piles of old row covers that have been used so many times that the tears are beyond repairing even with duct tape. There are the stacks of empty six-packs that the petunias came in, the hot-drink cups for tomato seedlings, the plastic flowerpots I've been saving, the empty black plastic nursery tubs, the assorted plastic trays and seed flats, and the hanks of plastic "burlap" from balled and bur-laped plants. All this is part of the nearly one billion pounds of plastic that is used in connection with agriculture in this country each year (out of more than fifty billion pounds overall).

Some containers I do manage to reuse — a few for sharing daylily divisions, or for potting up and starting the overwintered cannas each spring. I run the smaller pots through the dishwasher and sterilize the larger ones with a ten percent solution of household bleach (nine parts water, one part bleach). But my needs for these containers are finite, and our supply keeps growing. Over the past couple of years, I've reduced my inventory by giving them to a friend who has started up a small bedding plant nursery. But the old plastic mulch is another story. I have only two choices, keep it or take it to the dump, and the latter isn't all that different from the former.

I could escape this bind if my mulch were longer-lasting. Greenhouse growers cover their ranges with plastic that contains UV stabilizers so that it does not break apart after a single season of exposure. But every time I price this plastic it seems too expensive, and the dimensions seem too unwieldy for my purposes.

At the opposite extreme would be a plastic mulch that actually did break down, that was truly biodegradable. It is a plastic manufacturer's dream, a product that self-destructs — guaranteed obsolescence. The search for such a plastic is much publicized, and every advance celebrated. For example, mixing starch with the plastic polymers supposedly creates weak links that microorganisms can attack. But Cornell University engineers reported in a recently published study that when commercially available biodegradable films were put into aerobic and anaerobic digesters, disturbingly little weight was lost. As additional "biodegradable" plastics appear on the market, it will behoove us all to approach them skeptically, testing them ourselves to be sure that they actually do biodegrade in our own gardens. Plastic that breaks into tiny, innocuous pieces isn't good enough, for that means that we have simply turned the soil into a different kind of dumping ground.

A third alternative is to burn the plastic. An editorial in the journal *Horticultural Technology* defended the use of plastic by organic gardeners on the grounds that it could be cleanly burned in furnaces. But the way plastic is being burned today is in great, smelly, smoky pyres in open fields, not in furnaces. And even if it were being incinerated as a fuel, that seems an unsophisticated use.

The fourth and to me the most attractive option is recycling. Europeans recycle a great deal more plastic than we do. But we are beginning to tackle our mountain of agricultural waste. Dick Bonnett of Plastic Recycling Services in Parkersburg, West Virginia, boasts, "If you can grow a plant in it, I can recycle it." His company ground up and returned to plastic manufacturers nearly half a million pounds of old pots, packs, plug trays, and nursery containers in 1992 — "Only a drop in the bucket," he says. Sonoco Products in Hartsville, South Carolina (already the world's largest manufacturer of recycled plastic grocery bags), manufactures a high-density polyethylene film called Enviromulch. The company offers to pick up and recycle any that it sells, but the minimum order is several thousand pounds.

The necessity for large batches of material is a critical issue in recycling. Bonnett needs ten to fifteen thousand pounds of plastic stacked on pallets to justify picking it up, and the plastics have to be segregated by type. The spun-bonded row cover I use is PET — recycling code no 1. The black nursery containers are high-density polyethylene — no. 2. My mulch film is low-density polyethylene — no. 4. A lot of my flower pots are polypropylene — no. 5. And the six-packs and trays are high-impact polystyrene — no. 6.

All of these are recyclable, and all can be used to generate new raw material for the horticultural industry. The problem for the homeowner is that even a shed as full of old plastic as mine doesn't contain a truckload of any one type. What's needed is a good way to return these plastics to the sender. Perhaps the answer is to return them to the nursery they came from and tell the owners to give Dick Bonnett a call when they've got enough. I know of several nurseries that have already volunteered to take back empty containers, some for recycling and some simply to clean and refill.

The dirtier the plastic, the more difficult it is to convert into recycled resin. Plastic mulch is so thin that it can easily be contaminated with an equal weight of soil. That is why it's easier to recycle the heavier-gauge nursery containers. To make money, a recycler has to grind, wash, and dry the used plastic to produce flakes or pellets that can be sold or returned to the production line for less than the cost of virgin resin.

Some recyclers say that the technology for doing all this exists, that what's missing is sufficient demand for recycled goods. One way in which we can encourage the process is simply by putting our money down to support it. Buying recycled goods will complete the loop. One of the newer uses for recycled plastic is the production of "plastic lumber," in which recycled resin is mixed with sawdust or wood fibers and extruded to form artificial boards and timbers. Although this is a relatively new product, already some are advocating it as an alternative to pressure-treated lumber.

Pressure-treated lumber has become nearly as ubiquitous an ingredient of today's gardens as plastic. It is used for raised beds, trellises, benches, decks, arbors, always with the happy conviction that it won't have to be replaced for a long time. Like plastic, this embalmed wood is something of an artificial product, and like plastic, its use is accompanied by a good measure of public concern.

We don't use much pressure-treated lumber in our gardens. Our raised beds don't have any edging; when the posts supporting the hardy kiwi vines rot off at ground level, as they do every five to ten years, I go out into the woods and saw new ones to replace them. But I've worked with pressure-treated wood, and when people ask whether using it will hurt their plants, I hasten to reassure them. It won't do any harm to plants.

Part of my friends' concern arises from a confusion about the different kinds of commercial wood preservatives. The big three are creosote, pentachlorophenol, and inorganic arsenic compounds. The first two are used for railroad ties, telephone poles, and heavy construction timbers not likely to be found in a local lumberyard. This is a good thing, since wood freshly treated with creosote or pentachlorophenol will leach and give off vapors that are toxic to plants. Old railroad ties are an exception, because they have weathered for many years.

The pressure-treated lumber that is being sold for home use is so-called green lumber. This is wood that has most commonly been treated with a material called CCA, which stands for copper chromium arsenate. The copper keeps fungi from attacking the wood, the arsenic holds off termites and other wood-chewing insects, and the chrome binds the preservative to the lumber. Unlike wood treated with creosote and pentachlorophenol, CCA-treated wood doesn't give off anything harmful to plants. It can be safely used for everything from tomato stakes to cold frames.

The safety of the plants is not the only issue, however. Many people are worried about what pressure-treated wood might do to the health of the gardener. Copper chromium arsenate is toxic, there is no doubt about that, and its sale is restricted. In its liquid form, it can be applied only by licensed applicators under careful supervision. Homeowners who wish to treat wood themselves must use a compound such as copper naphthenate, which is much less toxic. But an extensive review of pressure-treated wood by the EPA found no significant hazards from the chemical once it is bound in the wood.

Anything that destroys the wood will, of course, release the CCA. At the EPA's insistence, the industry now warns consumers never to burn CCA-treated wood, to dispose of all sawdust and construction debris carefully, to wear a dust mask when sawing or sanding it, to wash exposed skin afterward, and to launder work clothes separately.

Lest these precautions sound alarmist, there is at least one dramatic example of the consequences of improper handling. In 1983, the *New England Journal of Medicine* contained a letter to the editor reporting on a rural family of eight who were stricken with a variety of symptoms ranging from muscle cramps to respiratory problems to hair loss. Their conditions worsened each winter and tended to improve during the summer months. When the fingernails of the entire family were tested and found to contain arsenic levels from 100 to 5,000 parts per million (versus a normal level of 0.9 to 1.88 ppm), the investigators began searching for the source. It proved to be the ashes from the wood stove with which the family heated their house, and in which the father burned scraps of CCA-treated lumber and plywood.

Pressure-treated wood can last a very long time indeed, ten to twenty times as long as untreated wood. A test series of two-by-four stakes stuck into the ground in Mississippi in 1948 are still sound, perhaps because this wood was free of heartwood and dried completely before being treated. The pressure-treated lumber we buy today frequently contains heartwood and is not so well dried. Not only does the preservative penetrate heartwood less well than it does sapwood, but as heartwood dries, it tends to check or split, allowing moisture to penetrate beyond the protective barrier.

Pressure-treated wood that rots away will, of course, leave its inorganic arsenicals behind, just as a tree that rots in the forest leaves behind its mineral ingredients. The collapse won't happen all at once, as was the case with the Reverend Shay's carriage in Oliver Wendell Holmes's poem "The Deacon's Masterpiece." Rather, it will occur gradually as the protective chemicals leach out. Where precisely the preservative will leach to is hard to say, and it isn't clear whether the addition of arsenic, chrome, and copper to the soil is significant. Morticians, for example, once used arsenic in preserving human bodies, and the soil of many old graveyards is well laced with it.

Some wood treaters offer a guarantee of forty years for their product — not a guarantee that every piece will last that long, but simply a guarantee that they will replace for free any that does not. Nevertheless, I think it is safe to assume that a great deal of this CCA-treated wood will still be solid forty or more years from now. It therefore also seems likely that a fair percentage of the lumber will outlive the gardens in which it is now being used. What is the homeowner to do then? Burning it is out of the question; adding it to the compost is unlikely to produce useful organic matter anytime soon; sawing it into short lengths to put into trash barrels will generate quantities of potentially toxic sawdust. The wood-preserving industry is beginning to address this issue, which will certainly become increasingly timely as people begin to remodel the home landscapes where so many million board feet have recently been used. The subject promises to be as complicated as the reuse of plastics.

Pressure-treated lumber and plastic, in the long run, seem to be related. Both are examples of durable products whose strength is also their weakness. Understandably, some gardeners find it simpler to garden without either one. Those of us who choose to take advantage of these materials where they make the most difference — the melon patch or a pier for the porch — must also take responsibility for the material's next incarnation. In terms of saving energy, of course, reusing something is better than recycling it. But it is better still to find a way to limit one's use in the first place. Someday it may be easy for the home gardener to recycle these materials. At the moment I find myself pausing. Once they are brought home, they are likely to be around for a long time.

SOUND ADVICE

Plowing with oxen is a tranquil pursuit. It's the learning curve that's rough. First there's the matter of steering. Jochen Welsch tells me, "Simply pull the handles to the left to make the plow go right, to the right when you want to go left. Lift up to sink the plowshare; push down to raise it." Then he steps to the head of his team. "Come up," he says, and suddenly terrible things are happening. I'm running to keep up and grabbing desperately at the plow, which alternately bounces along the surface of the ground and buries itself, veering off at a ninety-degree angle toward a row of Baldwin apple trees. The crowd of visitors hanging over the fence at Old Sturbridge Village are amused. The oxen, Zephaniah and Red Top, are less so. They halt and let me regroup. In theory, they are the ones who are doing the work. They are the ones shouldering the seventy-five-pound rock-maple yoke with its steam-bent hickory bows, its iron ring, the heavy chain, and the attached plow. If there is to be any sweating or heavy breathing, it should be theirs, not mine. I straighten the plow, and we start off again. This time I cut a furrow, sinuous to be sure, but at least continuous, running the rest of the way across the field at Pliny Freeman's farm.

"Whoa," says Welsch at the end of the field, and the oxen pivot as I lift the plow, turn it around, and position it for the return passage. Each pass of the plow across the field inverts a four- to six-inch-wide strip of soil, and with a team that has spent the summer feeding on fresh grass, as this one has, one should be able to turn over an acre of ground in a ten-hour day.

By lunch I have achieved a measure of control, if not mastery. By the end of the day I've learned that oxen are called working steers until they are four years old. And that a team shouldn't be the same size, since the "off ox," the one on the right side or the opposite side from the driver, walks in the furrow. Thus it is appropriate that Red Top is half a foot taller than Zephaniah, the "nigh ox," although both weigh roughly two thousand pounds. I've learned the exemplary disclaimer "I wouldn't know him from Adam's off ox," and I'm trying to figure out how to insert the word *boustrophedon* into ordinary conversation. (It refers to those ancient methods of writing in which lines

run alternately from left to right and right to left, literally as the ox turns in plowing.)

But the most important lesson I learn from my day as an apprentice plowman comes from the oxen themselves, and it doesn't even become apparent to me until the next day, when I am suddenly struck by how quiet it all was. Yes, my heart was booming and I was panting. But the oxen weren't. Welsch didn't have to shout his commands to the animals, or his instructions to me. We could hear the sounds of the birds drawn to the overturned earth, the chatter of voices from across the field. And when I'd got the hang of steering, which was really my only responsibility, the loudest sound was the susurration of the soil sliding over the iron moldboard of the plow.

We are so accustomed to being surrounded by the roar of traffic and heavy machinery that we find it strange to be in a water-powered sawmill, where you can hear the teeth of the blade chewing into a pine log, or in a vehicle where the buggy springs are louder than the *clop-clop* of the horse's hooves. Here I'd had enormous power at my disposal, an engine weighing a couple of tons, traveling at two or three miles an hour — and making scarcely a sound. It isn't the architecture that distinguishes Old Sturbridge Village, a historical reconstruction of an 1830s New England town. It's this quiet.

Ours is the age of the internal combustion engine. Its high power-to-weight ratio has made it the engine of choice for trucks and tractors, airplanes and automobiles. And these same engines power a host of familiar garden tools. I own a tractor, three rotary mowers, a sickle-bar mower, a rototiller, a thirty-gallon power sprayer, a shredder-chipper, two chainsaws, a brush cutter, and a string trimmer. I'm not a power-tool fanatic; these are just tools that I have a regular need for. Look in garages across America and you will find similar collections. The hitch is that these machines all eat gasoline instead of grass and give back not manure but noise, lots of noise.

The roar of a lawnmower starting up on a Saturday morning cuts off the birdsong, the rustling grass, the gurgle of water in the brook. At best the noise simply intrudes on breakfast table talk; at worst all conversation ceases. It seems exceedingly ironic that so much of gardening, an activity that is often described as an attempt to create an earthly paradise, has become dependent on making such a din.

Part of the reason we have been so quick to embrace the gasoline engine is that it allows us to tend our gardens with less time and effort. And so the push reel-mower has been replaced with the self-propelled rotary, the sickle with the string trimmer, the axe with the chainsaw. Increasingly, gardening activity begins with the first pull of a starter cord and ends when the last engine is shut down. "Mow, blow, and go gardening" is the term that Californians use to describe the proliferation of landscape services that roar through suburbia, mowing, trimming, and manicuring the grounds.

I can't hear the sounds of the earth when I'm running my rototiller; I can't even hear my wife unless she comes up next to me and shouts something in my ear. When the machine is running, I'm so wrapped in a fog of noise that I'm cut off from almost all others. And noise this loud doesn't just cause a temporary loss of awareness; unless I'm careful, it can cause a loss that's permanent.

We all lose some of our hearing as we grow older. It is a normal part of aging. Older adults, for example, can't hear the high-pitched sounds that children can. But exposure to loud noise is deafening many of us prematurely. There's no such thing as toughening our ears, no way to put calluses on the nerves. If someone says that he has become used to a loud noise, it is because he can no longer hear it. According to the American Medical Association, some twenty million Americans are regularly exposed to noises loud enough to be harmful, and some ten million of us have already suffered noise-induced hearing loss. They aren't all rock musicians, jackhammer operators, and jet plane mechanics. Some of them are gardeners.

The intensity, or loudness, of a sound is measured in decibels (dBs). This is a logarithmic scale, so that 80 dBs is ten times as loud as 70 dBs, and 90 dBs is a hundred times as loud. At one end of the scale are such barely audible sounds as the ticking of watches (30 dBs); at the other, the sound of firearms discharging (140–170 dBs). The danger zone for the human ear begins at 80 to 85 decibels, which is the noise generated by children on a crowded school bus.

Most of the garden power equipment that I own is in the 80 to 105 decibel range, but because I have no precise way of measuring it, I rely on a simple rule of thumb. If I have to raise my voice to talk to someone three feet away, then the noise of the machine is loud enough to be hurting my hearing. The louder a noise is, or the longer I am exposed to it, or the closer I am to its source, the more damaging it is likely to be. Although I can cut back on the hours of mowing I do at a stretch, there's no getting around the fact that I have to sit on my tractor to operate it. And so I try to protect my ears.

For this I have a choice between earplugs and earmuffs. Earplugs are those small inserts that fit into the outer ear canal. They must be airtight to be effective. Wads of cotton stuffed into the ear do a poor job, reducing the noise only by about 7 dBs. Good foam-cylinder earplugs, which can cost as little as a dollar a pair, can have a noise reduction rating (NRR) of 15 to

30 dBs. (The rating is printed on the side of the package.)

Earmuffs are larger and more expensive. They resemble the ones we used to wear against frostbite, only these are made of plastic with foam-lined interiors. Again, these have noise reduction ratings of between 15 and 30 dBs. Used in combination, earplugs and earmuffs will provide an additional 10 to 15 dB reduction over using either one alone. But neither will work unless they are fitted properly. When my own voice sounds louder and deeper to me, then I know I am wearing them correctly.

Rock musicians and their audiences prefer earplugs because they are inconspicuous. Gardeners, however, are less ruled by fashion, and I'd much rather wear earmuffs. They are big enough that they don't get easily misplaced, I don't have to fuss with fitting them into my ear canals, and they clearly signal to other people that I probably can't hear them. At our house we have half a dozen pairs, in part so we can outfit groups when we need to, but more so that a pair is always handy. When I'm finished with one machine, I just shove the earmuffs back and leave them clipped around my neck so they'll be ready when I turn on the next.

Protecting the operator from the noise of garden power equipment is one thing, but what about the public at large? Although the decibel level drops with distance from a machine, there can still be plenty of noise hundreds of feet away. This secondhand noise is every bit as irritating as the secondhand smoke from cigarettes. Noisy environments have been shown to increase blood pressure, change the way the heart beats as well as the rate of breathing, cause an upset stomach or an ulcer, make it difficult to sleep even after the noise ceases, and contribute to the premature birth of babies. Even something as commonplace as a single lawnmower operating in the neighborhood can have surprising effects. In one experiment, researchers studied the response of passers-by to a woman with a broken arm in need of help. When a lawnmower was running, no one stopped to help her pick up the books she had dropped. When the mower was shut off and the experiment repeated, people hastened to help her.

All of us differ in our tolerance for environmental noise. Certain classical music sets my teeth on edge, while some of my whistling does the same to others. But the one sound that has achieved almost universal unpopularity is the sound of a leafblower. Here in the East these machines are used principally in the fall, but in the West they are used year round. Their use dates from the drought years of the late 1970s, when California municipalities banned residents from using hoses to wash dust and grass clippings off walks and patios. In

sion regulations will be applied to outdoor power equipment. But they should be reminded that noise is an emission, too.

While we wait for listings of decibel outputs, the best that we gardeners can do is to test various machines before we buy one, paying attention not just to the weight, construction, horsepower, and ease of use but to the sound they make. One of the reasons that I like electric power tools, from lawnmowers to chainsaws, is that they are so much quieter than their gasoline-powered counterparts.

As for those machines that we already own, a little acoustic etiquette is in order. Don't mow your lawn before eight in the morning or after dark, no matter how bright the moonlight. Don't wait until your neighbors are having a party to blow out your gutters. Don't cut firewood on Sunday morning. And if you are called away to answer a telephone call, turn off the machine you are using first. This should all be common sense, common courtesy. It shouldn't require antinoise legislation.

Here in the country, where the houses are separated by a quarter of a mile or more, we can be more indulgent with the noise that we make. Nevertheless, I find myself periodically choosing to trim the lawn edge of the perennial border with a pair of old-fashioned sheep shears rather than my string trimmer. Or I reach for a handsaw in lieu of a chainsaw. It isn't just the prospect of the noise assaulting me or others around me that causes me to limit my use of power equipment in the garden. It is the way that the noise separates me from nature. I want to be able to hear the wind come down the hill through the pines. I want to hear the cooing of the mourning doves, the rustle of a chipmunk in the blackberries. These are the sounds of reassurance, proof that the world I care for is alive and well. The Amish have a phrase for this kind of gardening. They say, "We are the quiet on the land."

CULTIVATING DIVERSITY

On the main floor of the barn, between the workbench and the rack where we hang our shovels, hoes, and rakes, sits a great wooden trunk. It's a double trunk. Under the outer cover with its dovetailed corners is a hinged panel that conceals the trunk's tin-lined interior. Cool, dry, and mouse-proof — this is where we keep our old vegetable seeds, the seeds of gardens past. In theory, this is a storehouse of varieties, a vault of genes. In reality, the contents of the trunk are a shambles. If there is a lesson to be found in our muddle of seeds, it is that vegetable diversity is easier to celebrate than it is to keep.

The individual packets — some with colored pictures, others with plain text — are torn, muddied, and rain-speckled. They bear the marks of having been hastily reclosed by dirty fingers and carried about in a hip or shirt pocket before being dumped unceremoniously into the trunk. Here is a record, thoroughly shuf-

fled, of every vegetable we have raised or planned
to raise: 'Armenian' cucumber, 'Royalty Purple Pod'
beans, 'Harper Hybrid' muskmelon, 'Thai Hot' pepper, 'Detroit Dark Red' beets. The dozen different onion packets, still held together by a brittle rubber band,
hark back to the year we hosted the Olympic onion-
ring trials. An unopened half-pound of 'Silver Queen'
corn is a reminder of a spring when the ground didn't
dry out in time for us to plant this ninety-day variety.

Neither Elisabeth nor I consult this box often
enough, or we would have found the corn and used it
before we ordered more. We should long since have
inventoried the contents of the trunk and thrown out
the junk. Why are we still hanging on to my father's
'Yellow Plum' tomato packet from 1953? And even if the
'Green Globe' artichoke seed is still viable, haven't we
finally given up trying to raise artichokes in New Hampshire? At the very least, can't we pitch what has spilled
— those little black beads, the brown commas, the God
only knows what kind of squash?

The conditions inside our trunk are adequate for
storing seeds, but they aren't great. The seeds would
stay viable longer if we dried them down to five percent misture level with a silica gel desiccant, packed
them inside airtight glass jars, and then put those jars
in our freezer. We would then be careful whenever
we opened a jar to let it reach room temperature so

that moisture wouldn't condense inside. And we would open them as infrequently as possible, because fluctuations in temperature reduce the viability of seeds. Seeds are tiny living, breathing organisms. They need the right conditions or they'll die, and much of what's in our trunk is by now fit only for feeding birds or turning into baked beans.

I'm still proud of the blue ribbon that we won one year for having eighty-five different kinds of vegetables at the Hillsborough County Agricultural Fair. And we continue to plant almost that many each spring. Not only does this give us plenty of opportunity for crop rotation, it lets us do our bit toward conserving endangered varieties. Orchids growing in the canopies of tropical forests aren't the only threatened plants. There are thousands of varieties of garden vegetables that could disappear unless someone keeps them growing. The Harvard professor Edward O. Wilson, who has been one of my mentors, has been widely quoted for stating that the loss of genetic diversity is "the folly our descendants are least likely to forgive us." And some of that diversity is included in the vegetables that I used to carry into his laboratory as a graduate student.

The problem is that the vegetable varieties that aren't suited for mass cultivation or refrigerated storage, that don't fit neatly into containers, that can't be shipped long distances, that aren't dark green or bright red, aren't of much interest to commercial growers. Yet these oddball varieties are our horticultural heritage, a legacy of plant selection going back ten thousand years. The smooth-seeded 'Alaska' peas date back to 1880, before the appearance of the mutant wrinkled pea whose higher sugar content now dominates the class. 'Taos Pueblo' blue corn has been handed down from generation to generation by native Americans in New Mexico.

The term "heirloom variety" reflects the fact that many of these vegetable varieties have been family-held and -perpetuated ones. And many of them were treasured because they were so well adapted to the needs and conditions of a particular family or people. When you find a vegetable that does well in your specific climate or soil, that suits your palate and needs, you stick with it.

So why do we keep buying new vegetable seeds every year? Why not choose a variety and let some of it go to seed each year to start next year's plants? Partly it's because we are curious, eager to plant things that we've never tried. Also it's because I'm not sure that we have what it takes to do a good job of saving our own seeds. The problem is that most of the vegetables we raise are annuals. A few, like peppers and eggplants, are actually perennials, but we raise them from seed each year as though they were annuals. And seeds are a perishable

commodity. Squash and cucumber seeds can remain viable for a decade, but parsnip and onion seeds have a shelf life of only a year. Keeping seeds viable for longer than that means sowing them, raising the plants, letting them go to seed, and harvesting the seeds.

However, only the seeds gathered from standard, or open-pollinated, varieties will come true, producing plants that carry all the genes of the previous generation. And even with these standard varieties, genetic purity depends on preventing accidental hybridization between two different standard varieties. Accidental or deliberate, the progeny of such a cross is hybrid seed — a sort of gene soup.

Hybrid vegetable plants have been a boon to agriculture with their vigor, their uniformity, and the fact that seed companies can sell hybrid seed year after year to farmers and gardeners who are unable to reproduce it themselves. But hybrids are trouble for the back-yard seed saver who doesn't want to get into the process of plant breeding, raising generation after generation of some new variety of vegetable until once again it comes true from seed. For the amateur seed saver, hybrids are to be avoided.

Some vegetables, such as beans, are largely self-pollinating, which means that hybrids almost never occur, even when two different kinds are grown in close proximity. That is why the late John Withee of Lynnfield, Massachusetts, was able to maintain a collection of over a thousand varieties of beans, planting out several hundred of them in the same garden each year.

If the vegetable is corn or squash, however, which rely on wind or insects to carry pollen from male to female flowers, cross-pollination is a certainty. Unless the gardener is growing only a single variety and no other varieties are being grown within a quarter of a mile, it's necessary to take steps to control fertilization. Cages and blossom bags and hand pollination are all ways to keep seed pure. The recently published book *Seed to Seed*, written by Susanne Ashworth and edited by Kent Whealy, is an essential guide and reference for anyone setting out to save his or her own seed. Here is information about pollination, isolation distance, and caging, as well as harvesting, drying, and storage, for a hundred and sixty different vegetables. There are by now thousands of back-yard gardeners across the country saving their own seed, and they are making a very real contribution to the conservation of biodiversity.

Kent Whealy is the founder of the Seed Savers Exchange (headquartered in Decorah, Iowa), whose members — seven thousand strong — are dedicated to preserving vanishing varieties of edible plants. In 1990 he was given one of the prestigious MacArthur fellowships for his work, as was a colleague of his, Gary Paul Nabhan, whose organization, Native Seeds/SEARCH, in Tucson, Arizona, is similarly dedicated to preserving the traditional native crops of the southwestern United States and northern Mexico. Both men are passionate about the importance of these plants to the future of gardening — not just as a source of rare genes for future breeding but as plants that in their current form already contribute to a more sustainable agriculture.

As for my own reluctance to plunge in and muddy up the gene pool, Whealy allows that back-yard seed saving isn't for everyone. Given that ninety percent of vegetable gardeners buy their seeds from racks in garden centers and hardware stores, where the offering is limited, gardeners who simply order their seeds from catalogs are already doing something to preserve the diversity of offerings, as Whealy points out. To make this easier, he publishes the *Garden Seed Inventory;* now in its third edition, it lists all the standard (nonhybrid) varieties of vegetable seed currently available from two hundred and twenty-three mail-order catalogs and notes source codes for the company or companies offering each.

So what Elisabeth and I are doing is letting seed companies keep the lines pure, letting them test the seed to make sure that it meets the federally mandated levels for minimum germination. We in turn are creating a market for some lesser-known varieties, such as 'Mandan Bride', a multicolored, short-season flour corn that was once grown by the Mandan tribe in what is now North Dakota and that doubles for us as Halloween decoration and a source of whole hominy. As I see it, every such seed order, whether for white tomatoes or black radishes, helps to persuade the seller that the variety is worth carrying and thus preserving. We are doing something worthwhile even if we never get the seed into the ground. With this perspective, none of those seeds in the trunk have died in vain.

I will admit that we are perpetuating fifteen different varieties of potatoes — varieties that we have collected from people over the years, varieties with names like 'Ruby Crescent' and 'Russian Banana'. But these are vegetatively propagated. We simply have to replant the smaller potatoes left over from the previous year's harvest to assure a new crop that's true to type. We also have a dozen or so varieties of garlic, shallots, horseradish, Jerusalem artichoke, and rhubarb, but these aren't raised from seed either.

Although it's the exception among vegetables, vegetative propagation is the rule for fruit. The time we save by letting others preserve the diversity of our vegetable plot we more than spend in our vineyard, orchard, and bramble patches. At last count we had just under a hundred different named selections of strawberries, raspberries, black raspberries, blackberries. Also blueberries, cranberries, and elderberries, grapes and hardy kiwi vines. Not to mention peaches, pears, plums, and apples. In terms of the diversity that exists, we've only scratched the surface. But we are proud of them all, from the 'Brandywine' purple raspberry, which makes the world's best jam, to the 'Chenango Strawberry' apple, which ripens its fruit gradually over a month-long stretch, making it useless for the commercial grower but ideal for the homeowner.

Now that these perennials are established, they will all be here a long time. Some of them will likely outlast us. And there's a good chance we'll forget which is which long before our demise. This would be unfortunate, because from each of these plants, an unerring copy could readily be made by anyone. That is the beauty of vegetative propagation. The 'Baldwin' apple has been the same ever since the original seedling was discovered in Wilmington, Massachusetts, in 1793 by Samuel Thompson as he surveyed the route of the Middlesex Canal. The same is true of all the other cultivated varieties of fruit, no matter whether they derive from a chance seedling or from the most deliberate and controlled breeding. Whether the propagation is by grafting, as in the case of apples, or cuttings, as in the case of grapes, or the more recent tissue culture, used for raspberries, vegetative propagation (as opposed to seed propagation) leaves no chance for genetic confusion.

Where confusion shows up is in the matter of labeling. Once the name of a variety is misplaced, it is extremely difficult to get it reapplied correctly. Even careful scrutiny by an expert in the group may not prove definitive. Since there can be fifty years between a grapevine's planting and someone's request for a cutting, good labels are of critical importance. Records of what is growing where will let future generations know what things are.

The best advice, actually, is not to rely entirely on labels. Paper records survive far longer, and for safety you need two of them. One should be a map of what is planted where on the property. The other should be a catalog — a collection of index cards will do — with each entry describing the particular plant and including directions about its location. I keep ours in different places. If the map is lost, the catalog will still exist, and vice versa. Both are far more likely to survive than anything outdoors.

Peter Del Tredici, at Harvard University's Arnold Arboretum, likes to say that the limb you put the label on is the limb that dies. Every time. He doesn't know why. Labels can be attached to the trunk, of course, but then the tree may be girdled or the label swallowed up in bark. The smaller the plant, the more difficult it is to attach the label directly. But unless the label is attached to something, it tends to walk away, showing up where it doesn't belong or vanishing for good. Even well-intentioned photographers may lift a label and return it to the wrong place when they have taken the picture.

But first there is the matter of finding a label that lasts. Black laundry marker on white plastic fades, and the plastic degrades in sunlight. Wood labels rot. Black pencil on roughened aluminum is far more permanent. Our blueberries are all tagged with pieces of aluminum flashing stamped with a pin punch, spelling out the various names. The Arnold Arboretum uses an old Addressograph machine that embosses letters on a strip of zinc. Someday we might decide to buy a few of the engraved plastic labels that botanical gardens use for display labels, where the underlying white plastic is exposed by cutting through a colored layer. Or better still, the aluminum labels that are photo-printed.

Perhaps the most durable label of all has been devised by a fruit collector named Bill Vose in Paw Paw, Illinois. Describing his method in an issue of *Pomona,* the journal of the North American Fruit Explorers, Vose explains that he uses a thin wire to slice three-eighths- to half-inch-thick slabs from a block of stoneware clay. Then, after letting the pieces dry to a leathery consistency, he stamps them with the fruit's name, variety, interstem (if present), and rootstock, the scion source, and the date planted. Vose has the labels fired in a local hobbyist's kiln. Staining the letters with a dark clay slip and firing the labels a second time makes the printing even more visible. The weak point of Vose's system is the twelve-gauge plastic-coated electric wire that he uses to attach his labels to the trees. But barring a gunshot or other shattering impact, the labels themselves should be around for future archaeologists to discover.

Labels, of course, are useless without the plants themselves. For a guide to finding specific varieties of fruit and nuts, again we have the Seed Savers Exchange to thank. The *Fruit, Berry, and Nut Inventory* (second edition) lists all of the varieties currently available by mail order in the United States and tells you which of the three hundred and nine nurseries has each in stock. Alternatively, gardeners can turn to the even larger *Cornucopia: A Source Book of Edible Plants,* by Stephen Facciola, which identifies sources for three thousand species of edible plants (and their varieties), listing 1,350 firms and institutions.

In the end, even the right name is optional. Yes, the problems of synonymy can be nightmarish for taxonomists charged with assigning the correct name to a particular plant. Is a mulberry being sold as 'Wellington' actually the old variety 'New American', which was also sold many years ago as 'Downing'? We may never know. But saving the name isn't really what germplasm preservation is about. We can live with the loss of a variety's name as long as we save the variety itself.

ANIMAL RIGHTS
AND WRONGS

Living next to a federal wildlife refuge has its pros and cons. On the plus side, we take comfort in knowing that there will never be ski slopes or condominium clusters in our view. And we take pride in thinking that our own conservation efforts add to those next door. We would feel far more beleaguered if our hundred-and-twenty-five-acre parcel were a tiny wooded island in a vast sea of tract houses.

But there are also drawbacks. Wildlife refuges are intended to be sanctuaries. The problem is that their occupants don't always remain inside. The boundaries of this one are clearly marked by blue-and-white metal signs inscribed with the flying goose logo of the U.S. Fish and Wildlife Service. But there is no fence, just a century-old waist-high stone wall marking the four thousand feet of property line that we share. No one has mended the wall in generations, and many of the lichen-covered rocks have been toppled by falling tree trunks or heaving ice, leaving it of little use except to surveyors as a sightline through the woods.

The deer, porcupines, beavers, and snowshoe rabbits that have multiplied as the open fields have reverted to forest can't read the signs. Neither can the foxes, woodchucks, skunks, raccoons, squirrels, chipmunks, moles, voles, mice, and birds, which also leave the refuge at will. Walking, stalking, waddling, hopping, jumping, running, tunneling, flying, gliding — the traffic is heavy. Even the moose are back.

Seeing one of these long-legged, large-kneed beasts lurching through the alders like some misplaced camel is a naturalist's delight. To a gardener, however, it is another matter. I've seen what a newly planted asparagus patch looks like when a moose has walked through. I've had my raspberries flattened by hungry porcupines reaching for the tender cane tips. Deer have devoured half of every head of cabbage down the row and rubbed all the bark off the stems of my elderberries with their antlers. They have chewed the buds off my apple trees and the tops off my overwintering parsnips. The corn the crows missed, the raccoons got. Woodchucks eating squash, mice eating potatoes, squirrels eating peaches, beavers cutting down trees to build their dam — name the bird or the beast, and we've probably had trouble with it.

Judging from my bookshelf, insects, nematodes, and slugs are the principal foes of gardeners. Not here. Yes, I have my share of trouble with Japanese beetles and cutworms, corn borers and cabbage root maggots. But the damage done by these insects is modest. Even when there's the potential for it to become serious — say, with tomato hornworms — there's time to respond after you first notice that leaves are disappearing. With vertebrates, however, it's a different story. A single woodchuck can tuck away an entire planting of pea seedlings in a single meal. Raccoons can trash ripening grapes overnight. By the time I discovered that there was a porcupine in the orchard, my 'Montmorency' cherry looked like someone had been cutting firewood from it.

I am not the only gardener facing these problems. In Pennsylvania, New York, and New Jersey the deer herd is bigger still, and residents are discovering that there is nothing that a hungry deer won't eat. ("Rats with antlers" is how Princeton resident John McPhee refers to them.) Blackbirds annually cause an estimated thirty-five million dollars' worth of damage to corn nationwide, and raccoons have become so ubiquitous that they now steal even tomatoes growing in containers on city rooftops. The squirrels that bedevil birdfeeders are just as much a headache for gardeners. When venison, squirrel pie, and coonskin caps were in fashion, there were fewer of these animals around. Now, in our eagerness to embrace wilderness, animal populations have boomed and we are facing the consequences.

Despite the increasing seriousness of vertebrates as garden pests, most books devote scarcely any space to how to control them. I suspect the reason is simply that compared to controlling insects and other invertebrates, we have yet to develop many satisfactory solutions. With insect problems we can choose between resistant varieties, cultural practices, and biological controls. With bigger animals the choice too often seems to be between doing nothing and reaching for a gun.

The do-nothing approach has its charm. As a teenager and a determined naturalist, I put the rights of animals first. I thought that by planting more beans than we needed, I would be able to feed both wildlife and my family. But I soon learned otherwise. The concept of sharing with another species may well be unique to our own. At least, I've never detected it in any animal I've dealt with, certainly not the raccoons tearing through the cornstalks or the birds gorging on sweet cherries.

It became clear that I couldn't hope to harvest much of anything, unless, like gardeners of old, I reached for a gun. This was a .22-caliber rifle that had belonged to my father as a boy, at a time when lots of ten-year-old boys were given .22 rifles for their birthday and encouraged to go out and shoot things. At short range it was, and still is, effective, but you have to be close to the target — at least I do. I also began attacking woodchuck burrows with bombs, poison gas cartridges that I got from the hardware store. These cardboard tubes contain a mixture of sulfur, charcoal, red phosphorus, ammonium nitrate, and sawdust. You punch holes in one end with a nail, insert a fuse, light it, and stick the sputtering bomb as far down in the woodchuck's burrow as you can reach. Then, when you hear it beginning to erupt, you hurriedly cover the entrance with sod to hold in the toxic gas.

When I couldn't find either the animal or its lair, I set out live traps, baited with broccoli and apples for woodchucks, marshmallows or sardines for raccoons. At first I transported all the animals I caught ten or fifteen miles before I released them. I was, after all, despite any shooting and bombing, still trying to be kind to wildlife. Live traps are kinder than steel-jaw traps. But I was soon to learn that the kindness of live trapping is intended to refer not to relocating what you catch, but rather to the fact that you can release any cats, dogs, or chickens you inadvertently snare. Transporting and releasing a wild animal may condemn it nevertheless. Displaced animals have difficulty establishing themselves in unfamiliar terrain, and the more suitable the locale, the more likely it is to have a full complement of the species already. Finally, it was this amateur transport of trapped raccoons (by sportsmen bringing in quarry for their hounds) that precipitated the current rabies epidemic, which has recently reached New England. Taking all these issues into account, we should not be surprised that a number of states have by now made it completely illegal to transport trapped animals off one's property. This leaves the gardener to choose between admiring the animal and letting it go or dispatching it permanently.

I am not one of those people who stop their car every time they see a porcupine crossing the road and get out to club it to protect the forest. That's precisely the sort of knee-jerk behavior that created a need for wildlife refuges in the first place. Nor am I a deer hunter, though I wear an orange vest every fall for my own safety. I confess that I rather admire the man who hunts here each year with bow and arrows. The four deer he has killed in fifteen seasons of stalking seem an honorable reward for this extension of ancient indigenous hunting practices. But in general, I have come to believe that we humans are far less sophisticated managers of wildlife than the wildlife itself.

Wolves will probably never return to these hills, but the landscape continues to change so rapidly that it's impossible to say what the ultimate distribution of wildlife will be. In the past few years we've begun to hear coyotes howling at night, an eerie sound even more out of place than the appearance of moose. The coyote, along with the opossum, is an example of a species that has expanded its range, in this case moving east from the arid grasslands and deserts of the West into the territory once occupied by wolves. Coyotes are opportunistic feeders with a taste for everything from meadow voles to white-tailed deer, and they may prove a far better means of controlling the number of wood-chucks than I could ever hope to be.

When I was in graduate school, I had a professor named William Drury, who was an ornithologist and the author of two laws of animal behavior. Drury's first law was "An animal is presumed to be smart until proved stupid." Drury's second law stated the converse, "People who study animals are presumed to be stupid until proved smart."

These are laws that I have come to live by. What right have I to shoot every raccoon I see, or bomb every last woodchuck hole, without first knowing at least how many individuals are out there, what natural enemies they face, and whether they are limited by food or competition? We need to "quantify the in-fluence of both abiotic and biotic factors on popula-tion numbers of target species and their predators and competitors." That's how the authors of a recent report on the future of vertebrate management in California agriculture put it. That's a fancy way of saying we gardeners should go light on the shooting, trapping, and poisoning until we know more about our antagonists.

In the meantime, I garden not by force but by fence. I am like a zoo horticulturist faced with the task of mixing plants and animals, only instead of fencing the animals in, I fence them out. Before we sow the first peas each spring, we plant the fence around our vegetable garden. It's a four-foot-high barrier of one-inch chicken wire. The bottom edge is buried or bent outward, and the fence is tied with baling twine to skinny poles spaced eight feet apart. The top foot we leave untied so it will roll back on an animal trying to climb over.

This is a flimsy, wobbly fence, easy to put up and take down and put away for the winter. They don't make galvanized wire the way they used to, and it rusts too fast if left outdoors year round. Besides, the weeds grow up into it. Putting this fence up anew each year has proven to be much easier and faster than it sounds. Two people can erect three hundred feet of it in a day. It keeps out rabbits, woodchucks, and other mammals of similar size. It's important, though, to put the fence up before the animals start feeding. Otherwise you're erecting a fence on a game trail, and animals will go through almost anything to get where they know there's food. Even deer seem to respect the fence. They don't start grazing on the winter rye I have sown as a cover crop, or the overwintering parsnips, until we've taken the fence down, rolled it up, and put it away in the barn.

Raccoons, however, can climb any woven wire fence. The only way to stop them is with an electric one. Electric fences deliver thousands of volts at a pulse that lasts only a thousandth of a second or so. Getting shocked is startling to gardeners, children, pets, livestock, and wild animals, but all will survive the experience. A warning sign hung every two hundred feet is required by some states and will alert anything that can read. I surround the garden where I plant my corn and squash with two wires, one four inches above the ground, the second four inches above that. A good fence charger can be had for fifty dollars, and the power that it consumes is too little to register on most electric bills. For posts I use white fiberglass rods three eighths of an inch in diameter, and to each I attach two yellow plastic insulators that tighten to the rods with a screw thread. Since the rods themselves do not conduct electricity, the insulators are redundant. You can easily slide them up or down along the rod, however, so you can move the wires in order to trim under

them with a string trimmer. Grass growing up in contact with the wires could otherwise short out the fence. With this arrangement it isn't even necessary to turn the power off.

I have never had trouble with deer in the corn, but those who have report that a single strand of electrified wire twenty-four inches above the ground will keep deer away. The trick is to rub the wire with a cloth that has been smeared with peanut butter. In this case, however, you should definitely turn the fence off beforehand.

If I lived where there was a particularly high density of deer — some parts of the country have a hundred or more per square mile — I'd have to put up a far more substantial fence. Woven wire fences have to be ten feet high and can cost four dollars per linear foot to erect. High-tensile electric fencing has emerged as a less expensive alternative. Where deer densities are low to moderate, a seven-wire vertical fence, with the wires eight inches apart, works well. Where deer densities are moderate to high, a seven-wire fence that angles outward is a better alternative. In this case the fence is only four feet high but approximately six feet wide, with the wires a foot apart. Using high-tensile wire allows you to space the posts as much as sixty feet apart, and such fences cost only $1.50 and $2.50 per linear foot, respectively. The initial cost for such a fence may still seem high, but many gardeners have found that the security the fence affords their gardens is more than worth the price. Plans for the various types can be obtained from either suppliers or your local Cooperative Extension Service.

Most of my own orchard is surrounded by a six-foot-high sheep fence, originally erected to keep roving dogs away from my sister's lambs, but the three older apple trees in the back yard are unfenced. I protect them by hanging bars of soap from the ends of their branches. Deodorant soap still in the wrapper (I use Dial) discourages deer from browsing within a three-foot radius of each bar. At least it did until last winter. Now I'll have to try those "putrescent egg solids," or bags of human hair, or sprays of hot pepper sauce, or bone tar oil, or the fungicide Thiram. Each of these worked on someone's place, depending on how frequently it was applied, the number of deer, and how hungry they were. Repellents don't come with guarantees.

Fences, large or small, are a surer thing. The sheets of polyester fabric covering the young cucumber plants each spring are screening them against cucumber and flea beetles. Cylinders of quarter-inch hardware cloth or spirals of plastic around the trunks of young fruit trees during the winter keep voles from chewing the bark and girdling them. In the summer, netting over the blueberry bushes, grapevines, and even two sour cherry trees keeps birds from eating all the ripening fruit. The black polypropylene net with three-quarter-inch mesh comes as wide as seventeen feet, and sections can easily be laced together with baling twine or short twigs to make larger pieces still. For support I use a scaffolding of posts and wires. Because polypropylene will eventually break down in sunlight, when the net is not needed I roll it up on a long wooden pole and store it indoors.

The netting, the chicken wire, and the electric fence do an admirable job of keeping wildlife where I want it. Now and then a bird or two find their way into the blueberries or a woodchuck tunnels under the vegetable garden fence. Last summer a raccoon used an overhanging pine branch to drop in on the corn. I don't begrudge these animals their attempts to reach the fruits and vegetables I am raising. But neither does that mean I have become a pacifist. Being a gardener means raising crops and defending them too. I don't like bombing the woodchuck burrow that has suddenly appeared under the cucumber foliage, or shooting a porcupine that I discover chopping off the branches of one of my pear trees. But in good times and bad, these are the plants that I watch over. It's my job to step in and blow the whistle when animals get out of bounds.

....

A WINTER'S DIET

Sleet drums against the windowpanes, and the sanding truck has made its second pass up and down the hill. The wood stoves are all going. We have closed up the barn and sheds, oiled the tools, filled the kerosene lamps, and generally tucked ourselves in for the winter. We are like bears, we tell our friends: we're not actually hibernating, just sleeping a lot. When the sun comes back out, so will we.

Our bearishness is a matter of personal choice. There are enough heated swimming pools and indoor tennis courts within a short drive to offer an endless summer. And there is no shortage of fresh produce at the supermarket. For a cook, the seasons have become so homogenized that the calendar has lost its importance. Seedless grapes, celery, red peppers, oranges, and tomatoes are always for sale, no matter what the thermometer says.

We, however, prefer our version of winter. We like

the way our garden shuts down, the way the snow blows across the vegetable patch, catches on the dormant grapevines, piles on the bare branches in the orchard. For once, nothing needs picking. There are no pole beans getting too big, no raspberries about to drop to the ground, no broccoli in danger of going to flower. From March to September, from one equinox to the other, we race to keep up with what we are raising. Now, in the lee of the year, we are finally sitting down.

The last of our tomatoes was eaten weeks ago — the end of a bushel of full-size green fruits that I picked by flashlight as the temperature plummeted, then let ripen indoors. But I'm not about to reach for the tomatoes in the supermarket, even if they were picked and ripened in much the same way. We've had our fresh tomatoes for this year.

In part what deters me from buying fresh winter produce is the cost. Not the price, the deeper cost. It has been estimated that half the trucks on the interstate are hauling food or other agricultural products. In the Northeast, most of the fresh fruits and vegetables available in winter come from California and Florida. Some come from still farther away — from Mexico, Chile, South Africa, Australia, New Zealand. Winter in the Northern Hemisphere, after all, means summer in the Southern. But this long-distance transportation, whether by tractor-trailer, railroad car, container ship, or airplane, consumes roughly two thirds the amount of energy that went into growing the crops in the first place.

We also have concerns about pesticide residues on produce from abroad. While the alarm may have been raised by United States producers trying to protect their markets from foreign competition, there is no way of knowing whether chemicals that have been banned in this country but are still exported are coming back in imported food — not with so little inspection at the border, a crate here, a crate there.

What bothers me the most, though, about the fact that New England annually imports eighty-five percent of its fruit and vegetable supply is that this depresses local production. More and more of the grocery stores selling California tomatoes in December will still be selling California tomatoes in August, ignoring the tomatoes that are ripe in their own back yard. Roadside stands and farmers' markets are becoming the only way to get a taste of local produce short of growing it yourself.

Some of the growers hereabouts are trying to compete by raising lettuce, cucumbers, and tomatoes inside greenhouses, artificially stretching the summer season. But as enjoyable as it is to be inside a greenhouse while an icy wind howls outside, this is a marginal pursuit, given how much fuel and attention it takes to maintain temperatures so high inside walls so thin.

Not living in California or Florida, I find it simpler to recognize winter for what it is — a season without much fresh produce, a season in which our diet consists of food that has been put away for just this time. Here in New Hampshire, our family harvests from mid-June to mid-October. These four months sustain us for the other eight months. I don't want to give the impression that we are self-sufficient agrarians. We buy milk and bread, Brie and olives, patronizing the supermarkets as often as the rest of the population. But we don't spend much time in the produce aisles.

Instead we go into winter with a well-stocked larder. Quart jars of vegetable chili, spiced pears, dill pickles, and raspberry jelly crowd our shelves. These are not as elegantly packed as those on display at the county fair each September; nevertheless, they are summer captured behind thick glass. Canning has been around since its invention at the start of the nineteenth century by the Frenchman Nicolas Appert. Despite tales of botulism and pressure cooker explosions, it is safe, simple, and reliable. You don't even have to grow the food you can or can the food you grow. For several years now, we have been sharing our garden's produce with our neighbor Carolyn down the road, who would rather cook than weed. We grow it, she puts it in jars, we divide the result, and two families are fed.

Freezing is even easier than canning, and it comes closer to preserving the flavor, texture, and color of fresh foods — witness the superiority of frozen peas and beans to their canned counterparts. Clarence Birdseye invented a commercial quick freezing process in 1924, but home frozen storage became widespread only with rural electrification. Freezers have one great limitation, however, and that is that they continue to use electricity to keep their contents below zero. Every time I hear one of ours turn on in the night, I know the meter is running.

This is why the storage technique that we have come to depend on the most is common storage. Common storage is easier than freezing or canning. Electrical outages don't result in disastrous thawing, and there is no need to sterilize the food first, as there is with canning. Common storage works on the principle that a broad spectrum of unbruised and unblemished fruits and vegetables can be kept well simply if they are kept cool. And coolness is something that we have ample amounts of right now.

The best-known example of common storage is the root cellar. With so many carpeted, heated, well-lit, dehumidified basements, most homeowners have forgotten the merits of one that is cold, damp, and dark.

The ideal root cellar has a moist earthen floor and a temperature that hovers just above freezing. We had to hunt around with a maximum-minimum thermometer to find ours: the bulkhead entrance to the cellar. By lining the bulkhead doors with insulation and closing the interior door to the cellar, we found we had an intervening space largely underground that hovers around thirty-five degrees Fahrenheit. In the bitterest weeks we crack open the inner door just a bit to let a trace of the furnace heat into the space.

Here I store the one hundred or so pounds of carrots that we harvest in October, on Columbus Day, pulling their tops off and packing them in layers of damp sand in rodent-proof metal trash barrels. They will still be remarkably fresh-tasting, crisp, and sweet in mid-June. I am, of course, simply mimicking the conditions of carrots left in the ground. But the cultivated carrot, although it remains a biennial like its wild sibling Queen Anne's lace, has too much moisture in its root to withstand freezing. And those gardeners who have successfully overwintered their carrots by mulching them heavily enough so the ground never freezes often discover when they pull back the mulch that mice have tunneled down the row and eaten every one. Parsnips and Jerusalem artichokes are the only vegetables that we confidently leave in the ground all winter long.

Carrots, cabbages, turnips, beets, potatoes, and witloof chicory all go into the root cellar. The witloof chicory, or Belgian endive, gets packed in sand like the carrots, but the other vegetables stay moist enough in the humid atmosphere. I leave the stems and roots on the heads of cabbage. While the outer leaves of each head get papery, at the same time lateral buds along the stalk begin to sprout, and by late winter we are enjoying the etiolated, blanched stems and leaves of this second growth in our salads.

The roots of the witloof chicory I pack upright in sand, and every couple of weeks I take five or six roots, pot them up in a container, water them well, cover the container with a black plastic bag, and bring it upstairs, where the temperature is between sixty and seventy degrees. In a couple of weeks, fresh blanched chicons are ready to cut and serve. It may not be entirely correct to consider them a stored harvest, since, like the cabbage sprouts, what we eat has grown anew.

The ethylene gas given off by apples is supposed to promote the sprouting of potatoes; thus one is advised not to put them together in root cellars. And yet we know people who have gotten away with doing it. Perhaps the explanation is that their root cellars are so well ventilated that the ethylene gas never accumulates. In any case, we don't have enough room in our root cellar for our apples. Instead, we store them in the main part of the cellar, in bushel baskets and wooden crates. There the temperature drops as low as forty, and the apples keep very well. Apples for storage should be winter varieties. Our 'Stayman Winesap' apples ripen just before freezing weather but will still be sound enough for pies and sauce in late April.

Onions and garlic, by contrast, need an environment that is dry and cool, not damp and cool. I braid our 'Stuttgart' onions early each September and hang them up so they get ample ventilation. The elephant garlic and rocambole I lay in shallow trays. Temperatures as warm as fifty in the winter don't seem to harm them. Even if I don't plan on serving onions, I occasionally fry one up when I am cooking to whet people's appetites.

Our winter squash get picked at maturity and laid immediately in shallow boxes cushioned with crumpled newspaper or hay, so they are never scratched or bruised. The squash then spend a couple of weeks curing in the sun before being put in a place where it is warm and dry. Temperatures lower than fifty degrees, while fine for all other vegetables, cause squash to decay rapidly. The space under our bed has proven to be both easy to reach and between fifty-five and sixty degrees most of the winter. There 'Waltham Butternut' squash keep in perfect condition from one harvest to the next.

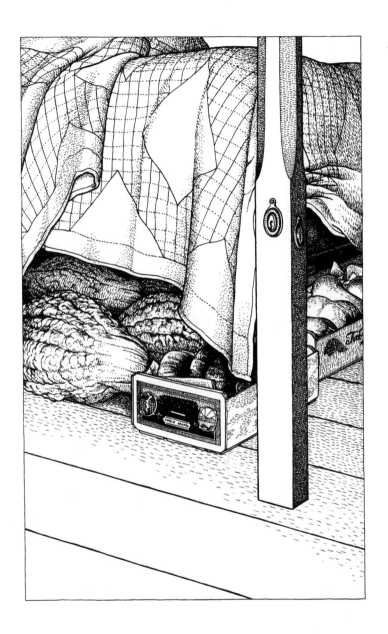

This isn't to say that a squash that has been off the vine ten months tastes as good as one picked more recently. But much of our stored produce tastes just as good as or better than what is offered in stores. Apples, pears, and even our hardy kiwi fruits do improve in flavor after harvest, because they contain starch that converts to sugar. Potatoes in storage develop a corky outer skin that makes them vastly superior to new potatoes for baking. We put several inside a simple metal box-oven set atop a wood stove and let them cook slowly all morning, until they are soft and squishy inside their tough, leathery shells.

Winter here is the season for pumpkin pies, stewed tomatoes, and onion soup. It is not the time to be buying strawberries, red peppers, or asparagus. Yes, by spring we will be a bit tired of potatoes, sauerkraut, applesauce, and New England boiled dinners. But that only makes spring the more welcome.

Every fruit, every vegetable, has a time of natural abundance, a time when it is both plentiful and tastiest. The diversity of recipes that exist for everything from fresh cucumbers to strawberries is a result of a seasonal glut faced by cooks. Someone who buys a precious half-pint of raspberries that has been air-freighted from the other side of the planet in January isn't likely to experiment with making something exotic like raspberry vinegar or soup.

Last summer we gorged ourselves on sour cherries, plunged into the ripe peaches, and emerged from the blackberry patch stained and smiling. These were all fruits that we waited to pick until they had achieved a level of perfection never to be tasted in a fruit that has been harvested weeks ago, handled by machine, and transported great distances. We overdosed on asparagus, sugar snap peas, and roast corn. And now we are curiously content. We still have plenty of good things to eat, food we grew ourselves and put away. The perishable delights of summer we remember perfectly clearly. There is no need to buy their pale, expensive counterparts. Of all the ways of storing food that have been devised over the centuries, the memory of past pleasures is perhaps the most efficient.

A GARDENER'S EDUCATION

Journal no. 3, July 15, 1975: "'A Brazilian is nothing without his farinha,' says Ceriaco, reaching his wood-bladed hoe across the five-foot pan to give the steaming meal another stir. The air is heavy and moist in the open shed with its low roof of red clay tiles. Outside, bright green dragonflies cruise in the glare of the forest clearing. With his hoe and a quarter section of calabash shell, Ceriaco keeps the farinha moving, gathering it up into drifts and scattering it back across the hot pan, until the wood fire underneath has baked and dried the farinha to hard, coarse, yellowish-white granules. Eaten plain, you risk breaking a tooth unless you let it moisten in your mouth, but that isn't how most Brazilians eat their farinha. Instead they scatter spoonfuls of it across whatever they have on their plate, letting it soak up the juices."

It has been nearly twenty years since I took these notes. I was a graduate student in biology, doing field

research at Fazenda Taperinha, a former colonial estate on the Rio Ayaya, a lateral channel of the Amazon some four hundred and fifty miles upstream from its mouth. Geographically, the lower Amazon is a long way from New England. So, too, horticulture and biology are not usually mentioned in the same breath. But the education of any gardener is an odyssey, as rich as it is long. Though I have returned and put roots into this rocky soil, the calls of parrots still resound. And I have come to see the farinha in a new light, not simply as a coarse foodstuff (though by any measure it is an acquired taste). Now I see it as an illustration of what I have come to believe should be the central tenet of gardening: knowledge can be preserved only by teaching.

This future magazine editor and television host was in Brazil to study ants, not plants. But when I could, I filled my journal with as many details of tropical life as I had the energy to record, from the hazards of walking through a Brazil nut grove when the cannonball-size fruits were falling to how the bundles of jute stems were retted underwater to rot out the soft, gummy tissues and free the fibers for making burlap. And when Ceriaco, a tenant farmer on the *fazenda*, invited me to help his family replenish their farinha supply, I felt I could hardly refuse, given how much of it I'd been eating.

The manioc roots, the heavy brown tubers of *Manihot esculenta* that his sons had dug earlier from a thick stand planted amid the charred remains of tree trunks and stumps, had been put to soak in a stream. Now the whole family of ten was busy peeling the roots, scraping them across the edges of machete blades to expose their white starch-rich interiors and ready them for grinding. The grinder, a wooden box with a whirling metal-studded piece of log inside, was powered by a crude six-foot wooden wheel with a hand crank on each side. The wheel stood at the other end of the shed from the grinder, and a slender fanbelt of twisted cowskin more than thirty feet long connected the two.

For an hour or so I helped turn the wheel, causing the younger children to point out that Branco, or "white man," as they called me, was certainly doing a lot of sweating. But it was hard work, and I found myself praying for derailments. When the cowskin belt slipped off either the wheel or the grinder pulley, you got to rest.

When enough tubers had been ground, the family set about packing the wet pulp into a long tube of woven basketry, a giant version of those Chinese finger traps that get tighter the harder you pull. This one was six feet long and roughly ten inches in diameter. Filled, hung from a crossbar, and stretched with the aid of a lever and a stone counterweight, it wrung the liquid out of the wet pulp, leaving it almost as dry as grated Parmesan. From there the pulp went through a coarse sieve to remove large fragments, and finally into the big round farinha pan. By noon the first batch of forty pounds was done; by the end of the day, two more, which Ceriaco estimated would last his family three months.

This elaborate sequence of steps does much more than produce the desired texture and flavor in the farinha. It also serves to rid the manioc roots of prussic acid, otherwise known as hydrogen cyanide. Manioc roots can be either "sweet" or "bitter," depending on the amount of two cyanogenic glycosides they contain, but the level of these toxins depends not so much on the variety as on where a particular plant is grown. Any bruising or cutting of the root mixes the glycosides with an enzyme that liberates the hydrogen cyanide.

From the biologist's perspective, this is an example of a plant protecting itself against insect or vertebrate attack. Bite into a root and the root bites back. But for a horticulturist, the story becomes a human one. I think now about how much trial and error must have gone into discovering that soaking the roots in water, cutting them up into small pieces, and squeezing out the juice removes most of the cyanide, and that the final heating drives off the last of the volatile gas. And once the discovery was made, think how vital it was to pass the knowledge along so that future generations could safely eat manioc.

Just the other night I spotted the familiar brown tubers between piles of sweet potatoes and turnips in the produce section of a nearby supermarket. There was nothing to indicate whether these were of the sweet or bitter type, and the woman at the checkout counter rang up the three that I bought simply as "tropical roots." Not taking any chances, I followed Ceriaco's lesson to the letter. I ran the peeled roots through my electric food processor, wrung the liquid out of the mash with a twisted dishtowel, and heated what was left to dryness in an iron frying pan. The result was a double handful of fresh farinha, as cyanide-free and every bit as tasty (or tasteless) as what we'd made that July day.

Some five hundred million people depend on manioc as a staple food, but the world population is more than ten times that and growing. Five and a half billion people cannot live on farinha alone. What we really depend on, all of us, is all of gardening. No human achievement in history has been as important to the survival of our species as the basic ability to manipulate the growth of plants to meet our needs. Call it gardening, farming, agriculture, horticulture — the differences are only a matter of scale and approach.

The deliberate cultivation of plants dates back at least eight thousand years and was probably discovered in multiple places on the globe. At the time the world population was a mere five million people, all of whom supported themselves as hunter-gatherers. Living this way, however, required vast amounts of land, a thousand or two thousand acres per person. Modern-day Chinese, by comparison, manage to feed themselves on only a quarter-acre of cultivated land per person. This is possible because our species has learned to garden. If the human population continues to increase, then even gardening will not be enough to save us. All our efforts to preserve the environment will be canceled out by inexorable human needs. And in the end we will be faced with massive hunger. But already, with a thousandfold more mouths to feed than were present at the dawn of gardening, we are absolutely dependent on the skill.

Gardening isn't just about putting food on the table, of course. It feeds our souls as well as our bodies. Ornamental horticulture and edible horticulture together keep our civilization from winking out. And thus it is no less important for those who raise roses than for those who grow manioc to keep the knowledge alive. Let even a single generation forget how to raise plants, and the consequences will be as swift as if we all ingested cyanide. Glassblowers have the luxury of losing and rediscovering their craft; gardeners do not.

This does not mean, however, that one has to begin

gardening early in life. The knowledge can hopscotch from age to age, up, down, and sideways. Picking up the skill at the knee of their parents may have been inevitable for Ceriaco's children; it is less likely when you grow up in the midst of an asphalt jungle. Many of the readers of *Horticulture,* like the viewers of public television's *Victory Garden,* are in their fifties and sixties. While a few can trace their interest in gardening back to childhood, most did not start until after they bought their first house, or their children had grown, or they had retired.

As one who spent his youth collecting butterflies, skinning roadkills, and studying to be a biology professor, I certainly consider myself among the latecomers. But better late than never, and there is something to be said for a range of experience. Think of the painter turned landscape architect, or the pharmacologist turned herbalist. These are people who bring new dimensions to the craft.

I still call myself a biologist. It helps me to think about the ways in which we influence the environment as gardeners. Plant physiology, animal behavior, evolution, and ecology are not common tools for gardening, but I have found them useful. The only thing that I really regret about coming late to gardening is that there is so much to learn and so little time for formal schooling.

Some of what I have learned has come from do-ing, and some from watching what others have done. More has come from the years at *Horticulture,* through whose in-boxes pass the experiences of thousands of other gardeners across the country. But the greatest source of information has been the very academic in-stitutions I once inhabited as a biologist-in-training, for it is under the auspices of colleges and universities that so much plant science has been and continues to be done. Had Elisabeth and I not promised each other when we married to forgo further degrees, I would have long since reenrolled. But fortunately, becoming a horticultural graduate student isn't the only way to learn.

The Smith-Lever Act, passed by Congress in 1914, was designed to help disseminate information from agri-cultural colleges, universities, and experiment stations. It established a network of agents who were paid by federal contributions as well as state and county funds. Though the original intent was to improve agricultural practices on the nation's farms, the Cooperative Extension Service, as it is now called, has become more than that. Extension publications, available free of charge or for a nominal fee, can be picked up at local Cooperative Extension offices or ordered by mail. They cover everything from "Beans in the Home Garden" to "Propagating Nut Trees," from "Leaf Composting" to "The Profitable and Sensible Use of Poultry Manure." But this isn't the only form of information to be had from the Extension Service. Across the country, in classrooms, fields, and greenhouses, on paper, over the phone, and on foot, Extension horticulturists work to meet their responsibilities of teaching, research, and education.

Unfortunately, a precipitous decline in the number of commercial growers needing assistance in this country has led to a serious drop in funding for Cooperative Extension. At the very same time, there has been an increase in the number of amateur gardeners like myself asking for information. The problem became so acute that in 1972, Dr. David Gibby, an Extension agent for horticulture in King and Pierce counties in Washington State, found himself completely overwhelmed by the requests for gardening information that were coming to his office. In a burst of inspiration, he proposed finding gardeners who, in exchange for specialized training in horticulture, would volunteer to spend the equivalent amount of time answering questions from the public. The program was an immediate success, with the newly trained "Master Gardeners," as they are called, putting in far more hours answering other gardeners' questions than anyone could have anticipated.

Today there are Master Gardener programs in forty-five states, the District of Columbia, and five Canadian provinces. Some sixty thousand people have been certified as Master Gardeners, after receiving anywhere from thirty to a hundred and fifty hours of instruction in everything from lawn care to pesticide safety. Although not all those who receive certification are active instructors, an estimated ten thousand are at any point in time — a considerable addition to the thirteen to fourteen hundred Extension horticulturists in the nation. Master Gardeners staff horticulture hotlines. They maintain demonstration vegetable and ornamental gardens. They help set up and run gardening programs in prisons and elementary schools. They conduct community workshops on composting and water conservation. They hold plant pest and disease clinics.

What is most admirable about the program, though, is the conviction at its very core that those who learn should turn around and teach. This isn't unique to Master Gardeners. It is what horticulture graduate students do when they become assistant professors; it is what 4-H is all about, and suburban garden clubs, and urban gardening coalitions. It is what Ceriaco was doing when he showed me how to make farinha. It is at the heart of gardening. All of us, young and old, must keep the knowledge moving. Gardeners have to be voluble. We have received far too special a gift not to go on giving it to others.

AFTERWORD

As his life was drawing to a close, Isaac Asimov announced that he had no regrets, explaining that "every idea I've had I've written down." But writing does more than leave a legacy for future readers. It also changes the writer. From a confusing array of experiences, the writer struggles to find meaning, the central truth, the consistent pattern that will encompass all the facts. It isn't the typing itself that produces the insights but the thinking that precedes each sentence. The planting is easy; it's the soil preparation that's hard. The wrinkled brow, the chewed lip — these are the signs of a writer at work. My computer, a machine by now so outdated that it is the amusement of the repair shop that services it, is still so infinitely faster at transcribing than I am at thinking that I have never felt any need for an upgrade.

The reward to the writer is that now and then the clouds do part and a flash of sunlight illuminates those of us who have been laboring down the row. These essays are an odyssey as well as an invitation. In my case, the sky-blue truth is that we who garden already have our fingers on the pulse of nature, and we above all must be doctors, helping to restore our land to good health.

But even the smaller flashes, the little ahas, that make up any larger discovery have been things that I wanted to share immediately. My father rose from his bath every morning with something that had just occurred to him, announcing it with all the enthusiasm of Archimedes. And I seem to have inherited some of his gregariousness. In return, I count as gifts the various letters, phone calls, and other comments that these chapters generated while they were being written.

One of these is an article from Jochen Welsch, the man who gave me the lessons in ox driving, which just arrived in the mailbox. It is a timely arrival, for it addresses an issue that pertains to all that I have written here. Going over these pages, I worry that my mention of root cellars and kerosene lanterns may be interpreted by readers as a sign that we can resolve our environmental difficulties by turning the clock back, by returning to a lifestyle of an earlier century. This is where Jochen's article comes in. "The Myth of Our Organic Past" is its title. "We as a society remain seduced by the icon of the early American farmer because of the ideas and the promises we believe he symbolizes: independence, thriftiness, and a respect for and a communion with nature," Jochen writes. "Despite what we want to believe, our agricultural forebears were not organic. Nor did they venerate nature."

An examination of the historical record, from tax documents and census data to farmers' daybooks and letters, reveals numerous deficiencies. Farmers and gardeners of the eighteenth and nineteenth centuries apparently planted virtually no cover crops; neither did they take advantage of crop rotation. And they did little or nothing to feed the soil. Manure management in particular was much discussed but rarely practiced. Most found it easier to buy more land when the yields of a particular piece no longer met expectations. "We cannot easily write off the effects of the agricultural system created by our forebears in the first three centuries of European settlement of North America. Their agriculture was neither sustainable nor organic."

Mythical or not, the past is attractive. To many it promises safety. Better a known devil, or a devil we think we know, than an unknown one. This is why the phrase "family values" holds such currency. But it is never quite clear whether the advocates have in mind simply home-cooked meals or something more sinister. Elisabeth, a historian, reading over my shoulder, says

REFERENCES

AND RESOURCES

EDITING LANDSCAPE

National Wildflower Research Center
2600 FM 973 North
Austin, TX 78725

New England Wildflower Society
Garden in the Woods
Hemenway Rd.
Framingham, MA 01701
Booklets on meadow gardening, wildflower cultivation, and propagation, as well as lists of botanical clubs and native plant societies in the United States and Canada

Richard Nilsen, ed. *Helping Nature Heal: An Introduction to Environmental Restoration.* Berkeley, Calif.: Ten Speed Press, 1991.

Sara Stein. *Noah's Garden: Restoring the Ecology of America's Backyards.* Boston: Houghton Mifflin, 1993.

New Tribe
5517 Riverbanks Rd.
Grants Pass, OR 97527
(503) 476-9492
Manufacturers of the Weed Wrench

145

THE RETURN OF THE NUTRIENTS

Firman Bear. *Earth: The Stuff of Life*. H. W. Pritchard and W. E. Akin, eds. 2nd ed. Norman: University of Oklahoma Press, 1986.

Eliot Coleman. *The New Organic Grower: A Master's Manual of Tools and Techniques for the Home and Market Gardener*. Post Mills, Vt.: Chelsea Green, 1989.

Robert Parnes. *Fertile Soil: A Grower's Guide to Organic and Inorganic Fertilizer*. agAccess (604 4th St., Davis, CA 95616), 1990.

Fred Magdoff. *Building Soils for Better Crops: Organic Matter Management*. Lincoln: University of Nebraska Press, 1992.

Raymond Poincelot. *Toward a More Sustainable Agriculture*. Florence, Ky.: Van Nostrand Reinhold, 1986.

Sylvan Wittwer, Yu Youtai, Sun Han, and Wang Lianzheng. *Feeding a Billion: Frontiers of Chinese Agriculture*. East Lansing: Michigan University Press, 1987.

E. N. Anderson. *The Food of China*. New Haven: Yale University Press, 1988.

Clivus Multrum, Inc.
21 Canal St.
Lawrence, MA 01840
(800) 962-8447
Distributors of composting toilets

BOTH ENDS OF THE HOSE

Robert Kourik. *Gray Water Use in the Landscape*. Metamorphic Press (P.O. Box 1841, Santa Rosa, CA 95402), 1988.

Farallones Institute. *The Integral Urban House.* San Francisco: Sierra Club Books, 1979.

Gardening in Dry Climates. Barrington, Ill.: Ortho Books, 1989.

Sunset Western Garden Book. 5th ed. Menlo Park, Calif.: Sunset Publishing, 1988.

The Xeriscape Flower Garden: A Waterwise Guide for the Rocky Mountain Region. Johnson Books (1880 S. 57th Court, Boulder, CO 80301), 1991.

Taylor's Guide to Water-Saving Gardening. Boston: Houghton Mifflin, 1990.

LOSING GROUND

Andrew Goudie. *The Human Impact on the Natural Environment.* Cambridge, Mass.: MIT Press, 1990.

David Pimentel et al. "Land Degradation: Effects of Food and Energy Resources," *Science* 194 (1976): 149–155.

Preserving Family Lands: A Landowner's Introduction to Tax Issues and Other Considerations. Stephen J. Small (P.O. Box 2242, Boston, MA 02107), 1988.

Samuel N. Stokes with A. Elizabeth Watson. *Saving America's Countryside: A Guide to Rural Conservation.* Baltimore: Johns Hopkins University Press, 1989.

Sam Bass Warner. *To Dwell Is to Garden: A History of Boston's Community Gardens.* Boston: Northeastern University Press, 1987.

The Garden Conservancy
Box 219
Albany Post Rd.
Cold Spring, NY 10516

American Community Gardening Association
325 Walnut St.
Philadelphia, PA 19106

ARSENIC AND OLD PLASTIC

William Olkowski, Sheila Daar, and Helga Olkowski. *Common Sense Pest Control.* Newtown, Conn.: Taunton Press, 1991. *Alternative wood preservatives*

Plastic Recycling Services
1001 Depot St.
Parkersburg, WV 26101

SOUND ADVICE

Outdoor Power Equipment Institute, Inc.
341 South Patrick St.
Alexandria, VA 22314
(703) 549-7600

National Information Center on Deafness
Gallaudet University
800 Florida Avenue NE
Washington, DC 20002
(202) 651-5051; (202) 651-5052 (TDD)

CULTIVATING DIVERSITY

Seed Savers Exchange
3076 North Winn Rd.
Decorah, IA 52101
Publishers of Seed to Seed, *by Susanne Ashworth (1991),* Garden
Seed Inventory, Third Edition *(1992), and* Fruit, Berry, and Nut
Inventory, Second Edition *(1993). A four-page color brochure
that describes the projects and publications of Seed Savers Ex-
change is available for $1 from the address above.*

The Flower and Herb Exchange
3076 North Winn Rd.
Decorah, IA 52101
A free brochure is available.

Native Seeds/SEARCH
2509 North Campbell
325
Tucson, AZ 85719

North American Fruit Explorers
Route 1, Box 94
Chapin, IL 62628
Publishers of Pomona

Northern Nut Growers
9870 South Palmer Rd.
New Carlisle, OH 45344

California Rare Fruit Growers
Fullerton Arboretum
Fullerton, CA 92634

Stephen Facciola. *Cornucopia: A Source Book of Edible Plants.* Kam-
pong Publications (1870 Sunrise Drive, Vista, CA 92084), 1990.

Carolyn Jabs. *The Heirloom Gardener.* San Francisco: Sierra Club Books, 1984.

Gary Paul Nabhan. *Enduring Seeds: Native American Agriculture and Wild Plant Conservation.* Berkeley: North Point Press, 1989.

ANIMAL RIGHTS AND WRONGS

Mary Louise Flint. *Pests of the Garden and Small Farm: A Grower's Guide to Using Less Pesticide.* Division of Agriculture and Natural Resources, University of California (6701 San Pablo Avenue, Oakland, CA 94608), 1990.

Michael Hansen. *Pest Control for Home and Garden: The Safest and Most Effective Methods for You and the Environment.* Consumer Reports Books (Consumers Union of the United States, Inc., Yonkers, NY 10703), 1993.

Kencove Farm Fence
111 Kendall Lane
Blairsville, PA 15717
Source of electric fence chargers and supplies

American Livestock Supply
P.O. Box 8441
Madison, WI 53708
Source of electric fence chargers and supplies

A. M. Leonard
6665 Spiker Rd.
Piqua, OH 45356
Source of bird netting

Mellinger's, Inc.
2310 West South Range Rd.
North Lima, OH 44452
Source of bird netting

A WINTER'S DIET

Ball Blue Book: The Guide to Home Canning and Freezing. 32nd ed. Ball Corporation, 1991.

Nancy Chioffi and Gretchen Mead. *Keeping the Harvest: Preserving Your Fruits, Vegetables, and Herbs.* Pownal, Vt.: Storey/Garden Way, 1991.

Janet Greene, Ruth Hertzberg, and Beatrice Vaughan. *Putting Food By.* New York: Penguin, 1973.

Paul Doscher, Timothy Fisher, and Kathleen Kolb. *Intensive Gardening Round the Year.* Stephen Greene Press, 1981 (out of print).

Eliot Coleman. *The New Organic Grower's Four-Season Harvest: How to Have Fresh Organic Vegetables from Your Home Garden All Year Long.* Post Mills, Vt.: Chelsea Green Publishing, 1992.

Mike and Nancy Bubel. *Root Cellaring: The Simple No-Processing Way to Store Fruits and Vegetables.* Pownal, Vt.: Storey/Garden Way, 1991.

A GARDENER'S EDUCATION

Local Cooperative Extension Service offices are the first place to inquire about Master Gardener programs in a particular state, but you can also write to this address for a list of local programs:

Master Gardeners International Corporation
2904 Cameron Mills Rd.
Alexandria, VA 22302

The telephone number and address of a local Cooperative Extension Service office may be difficult to locate. It usually appears under the city or county listing in the telephone book, under Agricultural Agent, Cooperative Extension, Extension Service, or USDA. In some states it appears under the name of the state university or college with which it is associated. To obtain a list of all the titles of available Extension publications, write to the Department of Agriculture information office at a state university or college.

The addresses below are for all the state and territory headquarters of the Cooperative Extension Service.

College of Agriculture
Auburn University
Auburn, AL 36830

School of Agriculture and Land Resources Management
University of Alaska
Fairbanks, AK 99701

College of Agriculture
University of Arizona
Tucson, AZ 85721

College of Agriculture
University of Arkansas
Fayetteville, AR 72701

College of Agricultural Sciences
University of California
Berkeley, CA 94720

College of Agricultural Sciences
Colorado State University
Fort Collins, CO 80523

College of Agriculture and Natural Resources
University of Connecticut
Storrs, CT 06368

College of Agricultural Sciences
University of Delaware
Newark, DE 18711

Institute of Food and Agricultural Sciences
University of Florida
Gainesville, FL 32611

College of Agriculture
University of Georgia
Athens, GA 30602

College of Agriculture and Life Sciences
University of Guam
Agana, Guam 96910

College of Tropical Agriculture
University of Hawaii
Honolulu, HI 96822

College of Agriculture
University of Idaho
Moscow, ID 83843

College of Agriculture
University of Illinois
Urbana, IL 61801

School of Agriculture
Purdue University
West Lafayette, IN 47907

College of Agriculture
Iowa State University
Ames, IA 50011

College of Agriculture
Kansas State University
Manhattan, KS 66505

College of Agriculture
University of Kentucky
Lexington, KY 40506

College of Agriculture
Louisiana State University
Baton Rouge, LA 70893

College of Life Sciences and Agriculture
University of Maine
Orono, ME 04473

College of Agriculture
University of Maryland
College Park, MD 20742

College of Food and Natural Resources
University of Massachusetts
Amherst, MA 01002

College of Agriculture and Natural Resources
Michigan State University
East Lansing, MI 48824

College of Agriculture
University of Minnesota
St. Paul, MN 55108

College of Agriculture
Mississippi State University
Mississippi State, MS 39762

College of Agriculture
University of Missouri
Columbia, MO 65201

College of Agriculture
Montana State University
Bozeman, MT 59717

Institute of Agriculture and Natural Resources
University of Nebraska
Lincoln, NB 68503

College of Agriculture
University of Nevada
Reno, NV 89507

College of Life Sciences and Agriculture
University of New Hampshire
Durham, NH 03824

Cook College
Rutgers State University
New Brunswick, NJ 08903

College of Agriculture and Home Economics
New Mexico State University
Las Cruces, NM 88003

College of Agriculture and Life Sciences
Cornell University
Ithaca, NY 14853

School of Agriculture and Life Sciences
North Carolina State University
Raleigh, NC 27607

College of Agriculture
North Dakota State University
Fargo, ND 58102

College of Agriculture
Ohio State University
Columbus, OH 43210

College of Agriculture
Oklahoma State University
Stillwater, OK 74074

School of Agriculture
Oregon State University
Corvallis, OR 97331

College of Agriculture
Pennsylvania State University
University Park, PA 16802

College of Agricultural Sciences
University of Puerto Rico
Mayaguez, Puerto Rico 00708

College of Resource Development
University of Rhode Island
Kingston, RI 02881

College of Agricultural Sciences
Clemson University
Clemson, SC 29631

College of Agriculture and Biological Sciences
South Dakota State University
Brookings, SD 57007

College of Agriculture
University of Tennessee
P.O. Box 1071
Knoxville, TN 37901

College of Agriculture
Texas A & M University
College Station, TX 77843

College of Agriculture
Utah State University
Logan, UT 84322

College of Agriculture
University of Vermont
Burlington, VT 05401

College of the Virgin Islands
P.O. Box L
Kingshill, St. Croix, Virgin Islands 00850

College of Agriculture and Life Sciences
Virginia Polytechnic Institute
Blacksburg, VA 24061

College of Agriculture and Home Economics
Washington State University
Pullman, WA 99164

College of Agriculture and Forestry
West Virginia University
Morgantown, WV 26506

College of Agriculture and Life Sciences
University of Wisconsin
Madison, WI 53706

College of Agriculture
University of Wyoming
Laramie, WY 82071

INDEX